Leah is brilliant! I couldn't stop turning the pages of **Your Royal Rendezvous**. Her deft pen is selfless and with one goal: to comfort, encourage, and assure the reader of God's ability to heal the unthinkable.

—*Michele Pillar, 3-time Grammy award nominee, speaker, and author of* **Untangled, The Truth Will Set You Free**

Through her own life experiences, Leah masterfully weaves pain, fear, and shame into the royal mystery of God's complete healing. She gently guides us through her journey of paralyzing spiritual battles, abuse, and crippling perfectionism and leads us into an exciting royal rendezvous with the King Himself. As we travel with the author, we too can join the personal discovery of the royalty we were created to be. Leah weaves Scripture, deep questions, and inner reflection to help us become all God desires. In these pages, you'll discover how to live inside the armor of God, what obstacles stand in the way of your intimacy with Him, and what it means to be transformed in His holy image. This is an exciting journey we can't afford to miss!

—*Dr. Susie Shellenberger, Speaker and Author*

Leah's willingness to be vulnerable and share examples of pain and fear that were transformed into victory is a tremendous example of God's power at work. This inspirational book provides significant truths on vital steps that must be taken in order to move into a deeper, more powerful and victorious life in Christ.

—*Lisa Blake, Executive Director Leadership Amarillo & Canyon*

Leah Fort has written a beautiful testimony of God's saving, healing, and redemptive grace! Prepare to be illuminated in the revelation that God is releasing to those who are ready to "shake the dust from their feet" and become all that Christ has destined them to be! You will want to read it slowly and take in the wisdom and insight of each line. Leah's style is warm, engaging, and her delivery is genius. God's divine anointing is on every single word! Take a royal rendezvous and be awakened to a life-changing journey of healing!

—*Donna Kyzer-Rice*
Elementary School Principal
Christian Motivational Speaker

Leah is a passionate writer exposing truths and helps for people who find themselves gripped in fear. The reader's eyes will be opened to the very depths of where fear can take you. Her honest approach leads readers to a soul-searching experience, identifying deep rooted emotions that have hindered them from reaching their full potential. Revealing viable steps of God's truths, Leah teaches us the way to freedom.

—*Sandra Porter, Women's Director*
West Texas District Church of the Nazarene

Your Royal Rendezvous

Awake from Your Slumber, Arise from Defeat, Acquire Your Place at the Throne of Grace

LEAH FORT

Paperback ISBN: 978-1-64085-829-9
Hardback ISBN: 978-1-64085-830-5
Ebook ISBN: 978-1-64085-831-2
Library of Congress Control Number: 2019911694

To Mike;
my favorite guitar playing "CR"
my reality check
my steady rock
the love of my life.
Together, we walk
through the dark nights of
heartache and heaviness,
and in the sunshine of
healing and joy.

Table of Contents

Part 2: Collapse

Part 3: Collect

Part 4: Convert

Part 5: Connect

Foreword

Having spent some of my elementary school years in California, I became accustomed to earthquake drills, rehearsing what to do in the event of an earthquake. If you are not familiar with the intricacies of an earthquake drill, it's a complicated process. When you hear the announcement that an earthquake is occurring, you climb under your desk in an attempt to protect yourself from the potential of falling debris from the ceiling, walls, or even the floor above you, doing your best to cover your head. That's it. While I have not lived in California in over forty years, and perhaps they have updated the earthquake drill protocol, I remember my concern about the threat of falling debris from above, from which apparently, my desk was going to shield me. But I was equally concerned--being on the floor--about how much closer I was to the massive crack in the earth beneath that I imagined was going to open up and consume me!

In our day and time, everything seems to be a crisis. If a massive tidal wave caused by global warming doesn't end our existence, then most certainly, it will be something in an artificial sweetener. And if we successfully avoid both of those, we will probably be doomed by the crisis-of-the-day that has gone viral on social media. It seems someone is always telling us to worry about something or telling us how we are to think about something or other people. There are many voices out there today, shouting about how to protect yourself from financial ruin and how to escape the nightmare of identity theft. Even our doorbells have been turned into recording devices because we can't trust people to leave our mail alone. One might get the impression we are living in a perpetual earthquake drill: get under your desk and cover your head!

Fear, anxiety, doubt, and worry seem to be around every corner. And unfortunately for too many, a constant companion from whose noose it seems nearly impossible to break free. But that is not how we were created to live. In the following pages, Leah Fort will take you on a journey. Mind you, it will not be a comfortable journey—but it will be well worth it! On this journey with Leah, you will discover what is preventing you from becoming the person that God has uniquely equipped and designed you to be. You will learn how to see yourself the way God sees you. You will experience breakthroughs and victories over strongholds in your life. You might even encounter God in a way you never have before. Doesn't that sound better than hiding under your desk?

In *Your Royal Rendezvous*, Leah weaves her testimony of God's grace, protection, and empowerment together with scripture and God-given insights to show how God has transformed her and how He can do the same for you!

It is easy to see how events from the past can imprison our minds with others' opinions, fear of the known and unknown, and the lies of our enemy, Satan. But take heart, there is hope! Freedom—from crippling fear, doubt, and the tragic events of our past—is possible. You can know victory. Are you ready to take the next step?

It's going to be okay.
You can come out from under your desk.
Your rendezvous is waiting.

Jeff Marcoe, Lead Pastor
First Church of the Nazarene
Amarillo, Texas

Acknowledgments

This project was in the queue for many years. More than fifteen years ago, I added this subject matter to my speaking engagements—my keynote addresses and expanded conference presentations. As I was invited more often to present it, I began feeling the Lord's direction to write it in book form. So, I started writing.

Through a series of crushing events in our family, I found myself having neither adequate chunks of time nor clear focus to download this from my soul onto paper. One afternoon, while awaiting the complicated surgery on our tiny, second grandbaby's heart, I had exhausted my prayers and was occupying my troubled mind by scrolling the web. My internet search led me to Kary Oberbrunner's newly released book, *Day Job to Dream Job*.

It was the perfect timing. I was wrestling with my career while also wrestling with our family's crisis. Kary was launching his book and promoting an accompanying conference. I ordered a copy of the book. After my purchase, Kary emailed me, personally inviting me to participate. I could not attend due to our family's situation, and Kary wrote to me again to say he was praying for a positive outcome for our family. Kary's outreach to me was both impressive and meaningful.

A couple of years later, I made the leap from my day job to my dream job (thank you, Kary) and afterward, I learned of Kary's new business venture, Author Academy Elite. I researched it, found it to be a perfect fit for me, and I enrolled. Today, you hold in your hands the product of that serendipity.

Thank you, Kary, David Branderhorst, and your team of professionals. You have each walked me through portions of this process by phone, email, video, online, and in person. You encouraged me to keep moving forward.

Enormous thanks to my editor, Gailyc Sonia, who set me on a more direct path with damage control for every poorly chosen word and sentence structure repair.

There are those who inspire me to move forward amid the darkest midnight, and against seemingly insurmountable obstacles, to triumphant victory. Those people include my sister, Carrie, my mother, Lillian, and dear friends, Leo and Rebecca Ahlstrom.

My encouragers. I could fill a book about you. You have a way of spurring me on, and I am ever grateful to you: My sisters since 1982, Janice and Phyllis, you speak life into all I do; Amarillo's First Nazarene Church Worship Team & church staff—life friends and Kingdom builders; Bernie, Christy, and Mary Lyn a.k.a. The Coffee Summit; Sherry Hughes, my sister-friend who keeps me in "Sherry Lynn Originals" jewelry; Bruce Hughes and Loyd Lanning, a.k.a., TLS. Where would I be without my big brothers?

Thank you to my children—Sydney and Chase, Lane and Neeley—who inspire me to do what I have dreamed, as I watch you pursue your dreams.

Thank you to my darling grandchildren—Benjamin, Bowen, Norah, Gracelyn, Merritt, Emma, and Viviann—who help me know there is laughter, joy, beauty, love, and hope for the future.

A huge "thank you" to my husband, Mike, for providing the space for me to write, in my favorite room at home in Texas, and beside our river in the mountains of Colorado. You are a prince for enduring all the early morning, all day, and late-night writing and editing marathons. You are the reality check I need when I dream and my steady rock when I'm in hot pursuit of my dreams.

Thank you, reader, for buying this book. May you awaken from your slumber, arise from defeat, and take your rightful place at the throne of grace.

Introduction

When I discovered the principles I discuss in this book, I was carrying out my daily habit of Bible reading and prayer in my time with the one true and living God, creator of the universe. I was reading in Isaiah, chapter 52. It was familiar. I had previously read it several times, but this time was different. This time it resonated with me, and the words came to life. As I pored over it again, I saw myself. *I* was the daughter. *I* was the one defiled, and *I* was the one in chains. Through His word, God was speaking directly to *me*.

But what was He saying?

I attempted to read further into the chapter but could not move past this section. Going back to the top, I re-read the same two verses repeatedly. My heart shattered before the Lord, and I began to weep. God revealed that *I* was the woman in this passage, and He illuminated the steps along the pathway of how He had liberated me from captivity. In His abounding love, mercy, and grace, God reached into my private prison and rescued me.

It is my hope and prayer that as you read this, you will open your heart to what God reveals to you about yourself. Just as God redeemed my mess, He will reach into the quagmire of your situation and create a transformation only He can.

As you prepare for the journey, I want to share with you the following sentiment:

Success, at any level, never comes to us.
Success awaits our arrival.

God showed me how to connect to Him and conquer strongholds so I could move forward into personal and spiritual success by taking my rightful place—the place He had designed specifically for me. God initiated my royal rendezvous. As you allow me to walk with you on the journey to your royal rendezvous, together we will unwrap the purpose for which God has created you. We will turn you in the right direction to pursue God's plan for your life and arrive at success as you fulfill becoming the perfectly faceted, brilliantly-colored jewel God has designed you as.

Awake, awake, Zion,
Clothe yourself with strength!
Put on your garments of splendor,
Jerusalem, the holy city!
The uncircumcised and defiled
Will not enter you again.
Shake off your dust; rise up,
Sit enthroned, Jerusalem.
Free yourself from the chains on your neck,
Daughter of Zion, now a captive.
(Isaiah 52:1-2 NIV)

PART 1

Confront

Awake, Awake

CHAPTER 1

Cavern Depths— Finding the Rough

The Awakening

Early morning. For some, it is a challenge. For me, early morning is a celebration of life. I genuinely enjoy waking up with the sky. Sunrise, hot coffee, prayer, and Bible study is the combination I use to begin a successful day.

While my children were growing up, they were not as enthusiastic about being confronted by morning. School days inspired me to awaken them with happy thoughts and sounds, so I sang my version of reveille. Each day was a little different, but it always went something like this: "It's time to wake up your baby bones, stretch your sleepy muscles, open your eyes, listen to the birds, look at the sky, and smile!"

My son would groan, pull up the blankets, and roll away from the light. My daughter was more verbal in her disdain for the morning. When she was eleven years old, out of her semi-slumbering stupor she said, "Mom, you are entirely too happy in the mornings."

Of course, I was happy, so I chuckled at her chiding.

As the two were closing in on middle school and becoming a bit more challenging to rouse out of bed in the mornings, I decided to implement a new method of initiating wakefulness. Rather than going in to awaken them myself—which had worked throughout elementary school—I bought each of them an alarm clock. I strategically placed the clocks in their rooms across from their beds. When the alarm sounded, each child had to get out of bed and walk across the room to stop the intermittent blaring and screeching. Every school morning, I sat sitting at the breakfast bar, my coffee flavored with the sound of their groans. Some days it required all my strength not to step in and turn off an alarm after nearly five minutes of continuous screeching. The great news is that it worked. The immensely unpleasant honking alarm forced them to get out of bed, and I was no longer the bossy—yet happy—mom, forcing their brains to turn on for daylight and confront the day.

As with facing the arrival of morning, the first leg on the journey to *your* royal rendezvous is to CONFRONT. Isaiah implies this concept as he commands in Isaiah 52:1, "Awake, awake!" The message is evident and emphatic. As my children experienced, when an alarm clock rings, it does not beep once and stop; it repeatedly beeps until *we* push the "off" button. It is as if Isaiah is telling us, repeatedly, "Don't hit the snooze button. Get your brain out of sleep mode. It is daylight."

Isaiah's words speak to more than the physical sense of awakening. They tell us to awaken from our spiritual slumber and wake up to what is happening within us.

Early one morning as I was following my daily routine, I read this Scripture and God set off the alarm clock in me to wake up and take notice of what was happening in my life on a spiritual level. He was showing me it was time to confront issues affecting my spirit, stifling my success, and preventing me from wholly fulfilling my purpose.

In my case, I needed to confront a spiritual issue that was getting in the way of every purpose God had for my life. How did this thing grow to be so large in me that God was showing me through His Word, that I needed to rid myself of it? To answer that question, let me take you back in time for a bit of a history lesson.

The Vertical Shaft

Confront. Confrontation. Confronting. Each form of this word seems to carry negative undertones because we associate it with aggression and argumentativeness. However, there is a positive side to confrontation—it also occurs when we are aware there is a challenge, choose to drill down, meet it face-to-face, and deal with it directly.

Being a visionary, goal-oriented person with a sparkling zeal for life and the potential for what can be, I laid out a five-year plan during my senior year of high school. The week following graduation, I began implementing my plan. I transitioned from a part-time to a full-time bookkeeper and salesclerk at the local music store, where I had worked throughout high school. I enrolled at the community college with the express purpose of accumulating as many course credits as possible by taking night classes while working full time. Doing so would allow me to save enough money to attend the state university located about twenty miles south eventually. Additionally, I started a savings account specifically to finance acquiring my own house. It seemed to be a good plan with attainable goals.

About six months into the plan, I was still living at my parents' home rent-free and feeling rather successful. Earning

$3.25 per hour, I was providing for all my purchases and car care, helping with some of the household groceries, attending evening classes, and I had already saved about $800.00 toward my house goal. Then, my grand life plan got scrapped when I began dating Mike, and six months later, we got married.

"The mind of a man plans his way, but the Lord directs his steps." Proverbs 16:9 NASB

Mike and I married when I was nineteen years old. We were enormously in love and wholeheartedly ready to be committed to each other in marriage for a lifetime. At the time we exchanged vows, Mike was three years into a career with a local energy corporation and was working weekends as lead guitarist and booking agent for his band, Crossfire. Crossfire was a group of excellent musicians who had been performing together for several years and had developed a large regional fan base. Thus, they were booked for virtually every weekend and holiday throughout the year, as well as special occasions. It was a reliable source of extra income, and the guys were all enjoying their success as musicians.

I was so happy in love that I rarely dedicated a minute of thought to the fact that Crossfire was the constant source of Mike's absenteeism from our home. Instead, I was busily anticipating his arrival. Except for occasions traveling with the band, I was left at home many weekends to do with my time whatever I chose. Therefore, I saved house cleaning, grocery shopping, and other errands for weekends. Throughout the week, our activities varied with the seasons. I worked at my full-time job (now the New Accounts Clerk at a small bank), attended college at night, played volleyball, and was a spectator at Mike's softball games and band practices. Even with the hustle and bustle of activities, we were together often and cheering for each other.

Amidst the activity and romance, the happiness of young married life and pure devotion to one another, I began to realize I did *not* like being at home alone all weekend. So, I creatively filled the hours of the weekends. The band was like an auxiliary family, and often the other band wives and I would go to supper, shopping, or to the movies together. I would alternate visiting with my parents and in-laws for hours at a time. (Later, I realized what a fabulous opportunity I had to get to know all our parents as an adult, and how through these times, our relationships morphed into our parents becoming my friends.)

Sometimes my best friends would come over, and we would travel to the band's venue to listen to them; gather other friends for shopping, supper, and movies; or stay at home and listen to music, cook, talk, perfect our makeup techniques, and laugh—all the things best girlfriends do. At still other times, my younger brother would come over and spend the entire weekend with me. I found a multitude of ways to fill my time with nonstop activity because I feared being home alone.

Even with all the commotion I created for myself, there were still nagging fears that crept up on me. Why did I genuinely fear walking across a parking lot alone? Why was I overcome with trepidation when I saw someone I knew from work, school, or church in the shopping mall—was I afraid they would want to talk to me? What would I say to them? Why was I terrified of sitting alone in my house while Mike was gone? Mustering the courage to get out of my car—alone—walk the driveway and sidewalk—alone—unlock the door and enter our dark, empty house—alone—was an act of rebellion against fear itself. Every time I successfully did it, deep within I felt a slight sense of accomplishment. However, going to bed alone in the safety of our little abode petrified me. I seemed to have an unexplainable, abnormal fear of simple tasks and regular events.

Finding the Vein—Changed and Chained

Until I married, I had never lived outside my parents' home and authority. My father was a Marine Corps Sergeant, recruiter, and an ordained minister. He was a goals-driven person and had a visionary mindset about the future (I am reasonably sure I caught that way of thinking from him). Daddy served as the senior pastor for a handful of churches throughout my growing up years. When not serving as an on-staff pastor, he ministered in other ways—teaching, hospital visitation, interim pastor, etc.

When I was in first grade, Daddy was the senior pastor of a church in a small farming community in the Texas panhandle. It was one of those quaint places people drive through to get somewhere else. Our town was large enough to have a main street with one flashing light, a grocery store, a couple of gas stations, a school district, a burger joint, one restaurant, and a few churches. Conversely, it was small enough that children walked and rode their bicycles all around the town, and people knew each other.

It was in this tiny town that I encountered my first royal rendezvous. Before we continue this lesson in my history, I want to define *rendezvous* and how it will apply to our study. *Rendezvous* is a French word meaning an arrangement to meet, especially secretly or under cover, at a particular place and time. It can also describe the meeting location.[1] The earliest usage of the word occurred in the late 1500s as a military term to describe a place for assembling troops, and the term remains in use today for military operations. As we use the term for our purposes it will take on both meanings.

One warm afternoon in the little panhandle-burg, the sky was brilliantly clean and clear, and the sunshine painted the day in golden happiness. It was a day tailor-made for running, jumping, climbing in and out of the storm cellar, singing, and listening to the birds tweet their songs.

As I was swinging around our clothesline pole, a random thought interrupted my play. I had a conscious awareness of Jesus asking me to invite him into my life. Instinctively, I knew I should talk it over with my father. I set out to find him, scampering through the carport and in the side door that opened into the kitchen. I walked through to the living room. On the other side of the living room was a small den, and as I made my way across, I noticed the glow of the television crawling around the wall. I edged up, heard the droning sound, and peeked around the corner. Across from the television, relaxed in the big brown chair, was my dad. Most days, he was busy carrying out his pastoral duties and working at the church, so I was delighted to see him at home. I inched up to his chair and said quietly, yet emphatically, "Daddy, I need to ask Jesus into my heart."

Daddy got up, turned off the television, and sat back down. He began to speak. I cannot recall the things he said, but I do remember him looking directly into my eyes as we talked out this serious and solemn occasion. Then he stood up, turned around, knelt, and putting his arm around me, pulled me close to his side. I followed his lead. We prayed together, and Jesus took up residence in my life. Immediately, I knew I was different, possessing new-found freedom. It was exhilarating. I left the room and went back outside to play. I didn't know it at the time, but I encountered my first royal rendezvous that day. The next Sunday evening, Daddy baptized me at our little church, and again, the pronouncement of new life gushed through my heart.

Autumn quickly arrived with its cooler temperatures, shorter days, and crisp evenings. Farming schedules changed, but the church stayed a constant. On Sundays, as the church building filled, older people gravitated like magnets toward their familiar seats while younger parents gently guided their children to the pews and flanked each end with an adult. The teenagers huddled, then sat in a group. One Sunday evening after the service, while all the adults were chatting, my older sister and I, along with our friends, were playing tag in the churchyard. As older sisters will sometimes do, she and the other girls ditched me and went back into the building.

Undaunted by my solitude, I found other things to occupy my time. My Dad had bought a late-model used Lincoln Continental (I'm sure a friend made a superb deal for him, since it was a vehicle "out of our league" so to speak). It was the biggest, fanciest car I had ever seen, and I decided to explore it. In those days, there were no locks on the steering columns. So, I could roll the electric windows down and up, push the buttons to move the seats and headrests, adjust the dome and opera lights, listen to the radio and eight-track tapes, and sink into the cushiony soft, black, satiny seats. It was marvelous for my six-year-old mind to travel as a pretend driver.

While I was busy driving into my imaginary adventure, one of the teenagers walked over and got in the car with me. He was a friend that lived a few blocks from our house, and he chose to tag along on my make-believe journey. Before I knew it, and without realizing what was happening, he molested me.

As this young man was exiting the car, he whispered to me, "If you tell your parents, you'll get in trouble."

He got out of the car, shut the door, and walked away.

I did not understand what had happened to me, but I knew there was something desperately wrong with it. I was petrified I would get in trouble over whatever *it* was, so I kept the secret locked tightly in my mind. When the teenager got out of the car that night, his silent exit slammed shut the cell door to my private prison.

Soon after that incident, I began having nightmares. I would drift into an innocent child's slumber, only to be visited nightly by the same terror. The dreams always opened with the same sequence: I was inside the church and running as fast as possible through the sanctuary and out the double front door. It was late evening. The sky was dark, and I could see the moon and stars. I would turn to look behind me, and there within close distance were two men chasing me. Quickly, I would turn to the right, run through the churchyard and into the side doors, run through the hallway and sanctuary, and then back out the front doors of the church. Like a hamster on a wheel, I would run this track over and over, glancing back to see how close my assailants were, and continue running. Each instance of experiencing this nightmare brought my awake, panting, sweating, heart racing, and often crying. It was horrific.

By the next morning, the nightmare was a distant memory, and I would get ready for school.

I enjoyed school, had many friends, and liked my teacher. We had a terrific playground with two small merry-go-rounds and one large one. The boys would let the girls get on the merry-go-rounds, and they would run and push as fast as their legs would go, then jump on with us as we whirled around. It was such fun.

At other times, my friends and I would stay on the blacktop and play hopscotch or foursquare. The blacktop was only steps away from the edge of the high school practice football field. One day, while we were playing at recess on the blacktop, the marching band was practicing their half time drills for the next football game. The band was moving toward the blacktop, and while we played our recess games, they marched closer and closer. My love for music enticed me to look up as they came toward us. I saw the slides of the trombones glistening in the sunlight and caught the eyes of one of the band members. It was the boy who had molested me. He winked at me. I was overcome with shame and embarrassment and simultaneously filled with hope that no one had seen him wink at me. Shame was something I had never experienced previously. *Why do I feel this way?* I wondered.

Sometime during the weeks following the molestation, another recurring nightmare began. In it, the sequence of events began with me walking down the school corridor on my way out to the playground. To the right was the cafeteria, and on the left were the restrooms. Ahead of me were thick metal and glass doors leading to the blacktop and playground. As I walked toward the doors, my friends and the other students were coming into the building from the playground as though recess had ended. While making my way toward the doors, I realized all the children were looking at me. More aptly, they were gawking at me. Some were snickering. Some were whispering, pointing toward me and then giggling. When I realized they were looking at me, I would look down to see what was wrong.

At this point, the dream would play out in one of two ways. In one scene, I found I was walking through the school wearing only my panties and slip. In the second scenario, I saw myself naked. In both scenarios, I was still wearing my socks and shoes. At that moment in the dream, I would run into the restroom, mortified and crying because everyone saw me like that. Then, I would awaken, teary and out of breath.

This second dream reveals that although I did not have full awareness and understanding of what was done to me that fateful evening after church, I had a deep sense of shame about myself and my body. The shame played out in my nightmare when I ran away from my friends to hide in the restroom.

I share these nightmares and reveal their nature with you to help you understand that while the assault happened one time, it nevertheless had a profound and lifelong effect. There are some reading this account who have endured much more horrific circumstances and my heart grieves for your pain.

Trust and Purpose

Thankfully, in all this there is also good news. God, in His infinite wisdom, had already made His investment in me. It was only weeks before the wicked misdeed that I had my first encounter with the King and had chosen to trust and follow Jesus Christ. I belonged to God. While we live in this fallen world of sin and error, trials and tribulations, and are subjected to things not always of our choosing, God has created each of us with a purpose to fulfill.

> For you created my inmost being;
> you knit me together in my mother's womb.
> I praise you because I am fearfully and wonderfully made;
> your works are wonderful,
> I know that full well.
> My frame was not hidden from you
> when I was made in the secret place,
> when I was woven together in the depths of the earth.
> Your eyes saw my unformed body;
> all the days ordained for me were written in your book
> before one of them came to be.
> How precious to me are your thoughts, God!
> How vast is the sum of them!
> Were I to count them,
> they would outnumber the grains of sand—
> when I awake, I am still with you. (Ps. 139:13-18)

Every time I experienced those nightmares, God was still with me when I awoke. I still belonged to him.

Reflecting on these times in my history, God was awakening me to awareness—awareness of Him, ever-present and working in my spirit. Knowledge of things in my life that needed to change, God showed me how to meet Him at the jeweler's bench, conquer fear, and find success.

As we continue our mining and discovery, I will share other pieces of my story, and you will begin to insert yourself into the process of this royal rendezvous. As you progress, my goal is to help guide you along your journey. With the support of Scripture, I will help you wake up to what is happening within yourself so you can identify the issues preventing you from wholly fulfilling the purpose for which God has created you. I will point you to what God says you can do to confront and remove those hindrances from your life so you can become all God created you to be.

So, join me as we set out on the quest for *your* royal rendezvous, and no matter what time it is where you are, you can awake from your slumber, arise from defeat, and acquire your place at the throne of grace.

Glimmers of the Crown

Our most powerful moments are when we face, head-on, what binds us and prohibits us from reaching our full potential for spiritual and personal success. Such moments come when we lay our hearts before the Lord and without reservation ask Him to reveal to us the reality of our condition. To aid in your quest as you begin your journey, following is a prayer I prepared to help guide you in seeking the Lord's direction.

Lord, I thank you that you love me and that because of your love, you want me, and my life, to be more like you. I am on a journey to be connected you fully, and it seems my life may be a wreck in some areas because of a disconnection from you. I need to know the areas I am out of your order for my life. As I move forward, I want you to show me the places that are strongholds in my life. I ask you, Lord, to bring into focus the flaws of this heart that longs to be your brilliant jewel. Help me, as I begin to see these flaws of strongholds, to acknowledge the truth about what is in me that needs to be culled. Like the hammer of a jeweler, let your spirit break open my heart and mind to gems that take on your light. Help me have a teachable spirit to hear your voice and change the things you show me, that each facet will dance with the colors of you. I thank you for your Holy Spirit at work in me.

CHAPTER 2

From the Ground—Out of the Mine

At my awakening God began revealing changes I needed to make. The first part of this change was to be aware of what was happening in my life on a spiritual level and to confront that. Like a rough slab mined from the ground, I was a hewn stone coming out of the depths of a stale and lifeless entombment.

Growth requires change. God enables us to see the real problem so we can confront those issues in our lives which are creating the need for spiritual re-awakening. Then it is up to us to act.

In my case, I was a jewel vein entombed in the hardened sediment of fear. I was trapped under a ledge of suffocating dread and needed to confront the fear. It was time to set the charge and blast away every doubt clinging to me, whether trepidations, feeling of sinister foreboding, or overwhelm. Because of things perpetrated upon me as a young child, I was able to identify the origin of this ghastly beast and attack it directly.

A New Kind of Normal

As I continue with the history lesson from my life, we will leap forward about three years. By my ninth birthday, we had moved back to Amarillo, Texas.[2] Amarillo, a small, family-friendly city located in the center of the southern United States, became home base for us. My dad was not serving in a full-time pastoral position at that time but was working a regular job and doing interim pastorate work for churches throughout the Texas panhandle. Most of the time, we attended a large church located in Amarillo's central business district on Route 66.

Summer arrived after third grade, and my best church friend, Cathy, and I were preparing to attend church camp. It would be my first year to take part in a camp that my parents were not also attending or helping with some portion. I was exceedingly excited about this new independence.

We arrived at the camp, as did the intense heat of summer. The camp was in Roaring Springs, Texas. I remember it more as a roaring desert campground, complete with a few uninvited guests—scorpions. That aside, it was camp, and there was fun to be found. We swam. We sang. We sang "Get Your Elbows Off the Table" to those who were ever-so-rude to break dining etiquette. All week, there was growing anticipation of the daring "midnight hike." For primary camp, we embarked on the hike at about ten o'clock, but it was a nighttime adventure, sure to be filled with excitement.

Following all the daytime events and activities, each evening of camp we prepared for the church service, known as *tabernacle*. It was a dress-up event where the girls wore dresses, and the boys traded in tee shirts and play jeans for button-down shirts and slacks. We excitedly chattered as we prepared for the first night of tabernacle. We ensured we had our Bibles before leaving the dormitories, as well as coins for children's missions offering and extra money for a scrumptiously sweet treat from the snack-shack after service. We continued with our chatter and strolled eagerly to the screened in chapel. It was perfectly appointed for us. The chapel was painted white and had child-sized chairs and altars, a puppet stage, and a speaker's podium.

We sang, watched a puppet show, and had a special children's speaker on the first night of camp. While I do not recall the content of the puppet program or the speaker's words, as I sat in the end seat with the center aisle to my right, there was a compelling in my spirit that would not stop. I was eagerly anticipating an invitation for prayer at the altars, and when that moment arrived, I made a beeline to the altar.

I knelt and began talking aloud to God. My conversation with the Almighty obscured my awareness of others. It seemed there was nobody in the room but me. I felt compelled from deep within, a prompting of the Lord, to raise my hands. As I lifted my hands, God's Holy Spirit poured over me, and I was praying with great fervor. I use the term *poured* because it was as if something touched the top of my head and trickled over and throughout my entire being. I was praying with an intensity and fervor of which I was unaware before that moment. The Holy Spirit was pouring Himself into me, and I was ready.

The following three nights of camp, I enthusiastically awaited the moment the altars were opened. I could not get enough of the outpouring of God's Spirit into mine. Inside, I was brand new. I was different. There were no words to explain adequately this heart alteration. I knew my very essence was in the midst of transformation.

Friday morning arrived. We bid farewell to our newfound camp friends and boarded our buses to reenter our ordinary lives. However, for me, I was living a new normal. My spirit was changed.

Accosted Adventure to Another Normal

As school began my fifth-grade year, I said *so long* to summer in eager anticipation of the arrival of the Tri-State Fair, high school football season, and the chili supper and carnival at the elementary school.

My next-door neighbor, Deborah, and I were the same age. We spent lots of time together, in and out of each other's homes, riding bikes, playing dolls, and listening to records. Deborah's family had a bit of a different lifestyle than mine. Her mother bowled in a league which took her traveling in tours all over the United States. Deborah's stepfather was the general manager and chief cook of the grill at the bowling alley located approximately one mile east of our houses. When we wanted a real adventure, Deborah and I would walk to the bowling alley and share a plate of fries and a bottle of Fresca. They were free to us, and we thought that was fantastic.

Late one afternoon, Deborah and I had no homework, and we were bored. We headed to the bowling alley for a treat. Still dressed in our school clothes, using extra care and extra napkins, we gobbled our ketchup-laden fries and opened the huge kitchen cooler for a cold drink. We roamed through the dining area, then scoured the bowling alley to check for friends who might be bowling or in the arcade. No one. We decided to walk to the convenience store a couple of blocks south to get some candy.

With candy in hand—and in our mouths—we strolled back toward the bowling alley. At the corner, just across from the grill's kitchen door, Deborah commanded, "Leah, run!"

Puzzled, I turned to her and said, "What?"

Frightened, Deborah yelled, "Run!" and bolted toward the grill's kitchen door.

A bit dazed by her behavior, I turned straight forward. In the bowling alley parking lot, was a large bronze-colored sedan, with the driver's window open. A man was in the driver's seat with his wavy, black-haired, pompadoured head sticking out the window.

Speaking in a powerfully gruff voice, he hollered, "I said, "Come here!"

Stunned, I watched as this stranger hit the accelerator and screeched out of the parking lot. He stopped directly in front of me, blocking my way. He opened the door and popped out of the car. Driver's door still open, he grabbed me with the express intention of forcing me into the vehicle.

As he held tightly to my left arm, he pushed my head to turn and manipulate my body toward the inside of the car. I was facing him and fighting against him. His shiny, black cowboy boots were sticking out from under his indigo jeans.

Bobbing my head in the struggle to get loose from his grip, I saw his belt and black shirt. I caught extended glimpses of his slick and wavy pompadour. The green lenses of his horn-rimmed sunglasses partially covered his deeply tanned and angry face.

His grip tightened. He was gritting his teeth and grunting, trying to force me into the vehicle. With equal volition, I fought to avoid the interior of that car. As I struggled, I turned and saw Deborah peeking around the corner from the grill's kitchen door, her bright blue eyes stretched like skillets. I wanted to be inside the security of that familiar kitchen.

My attention instantly returned to what I now know was a fight for my life. I kicked. I pulled. I pushed. I wrestled. In the battle, I was finally able to free my arm while he tried to regain his hold on me. I escaped his grasp. As I pulled away from his claw-like clutch, his fingernails, like talons, raked down and around my left forearm, leaving scrapes oozing tiny droplets of blood.

I saw the kitchen steps and knew if I got inside, everything would be all right. I do not remember my feet touching the ground. I only remember being nearly thrust inside that huge car, and then I was running up the steps to the kitchen door. I grabbed the handle on the wooden screen door and plunged my feet into that greasy sanctuary. The screen door slapped closed hard behind me. Deborah and I were terrified and crying, then we suddenly stopped. Shock set in quickly.

Once inside the dining area, a few steps up from the bowling lanes, seemingly out of nowhere, a police officer was quietly and kindly bending toward me, asking me questions about the incident. While she was talking to me, two silhouettes were moving toward me as the west sun shone through the glass doors behind them. I peeked around the police officer, and as my eyes adjusted to the brightness of the sunlight, I saw my parents trotting through the lobby toward me. I remember the relief I felt at seeing them, even though I was still terrified.

Strangely weak, I could not jump up to hug them. As my parents began speaking with the police officer, I sat numbly. I heard the drone of their voices without hearing their words.

I was a small ten-year-old, and there is no explanation—other than the grace of God—for how I was able to escape my assailant.

Word of the incident made its way around school quickly. Interestingly, only a few of my friends asked me questions about it. Most of our friends directed their questions to Deborah. When I recall that time, our friends were probably too disconcerted to ask me directly. We lived in a quiet and close-knit community, and the thought of something so dastardly happening—especially to one of their own—was too frightening.

Although circumstances in my early years seemed to create an upstream torrent flowing against me, I was somehow able to move past these terrors and live a mostly normal childhood. I played on a softball team throughout elementary school, and since I was not the best hitter, I learned how to run fast. We were city champs several times, thanks to our star players, Celine, Rhonda, and Patty—respectively, the best elementary pitcher, first, and third basemen you could hope to have on your team. In the first game Celine pitched, we run-ruled the other side, with a winning score of 39-0. It was also the season another excellent softball player would become my lifelong dear friend, Robin.

I took piano lessons for a few years, played the flute in band and orchestra, sang in the choir, and sang and played in duets and various ensembles, earning UIL Division 1 medals. I did all those things throughout school, and took part in the similar church happenings, as well.

My friends and I enjoyed getting on our bicycles and riding miles and miles all over our part of town. On weekends, Robin and I would ask for extra money so we could ride our bikes to the closest pizzeria, where we would get a pepperoni pizza, load it with parmesan cheese, and drink Cokes (in Texas, all soft drinks are called "Coke"). We learned the bus routes and decided it would be great fun to take the bus downtown and go shopping. Our bus tour took us to the biggest sporting goods store, the locally owned Vance Hall's Sporting Goods, where we bought baseball sleeve shirts in our junior high school colors, and had our names lettered on them. We received many accolades at the next all-school dance with our matching shirts and our story of the bus adventure. For a couple of weeks, we were the talk of some of our seventh-grade friends, as well as some kids in the upper grades. In our minds, it was a colossal adventure for a couple of twelve-year-old kids to take the bus from the farthest southeast part of our city to the downtown central business district.

My family lived about a mile southwest of our junior high school, and I walked home most days with a large group of kids. We each saved our lunch change all week so on Fridays we could stop at the pizzeria to get a Coke, play records on the jukebox, and dance for a while before walking the rest of the way home. Those were indeed some of my favorite times in junior high.

I consider myself fortunate to have been taught by highly demanding teachers in all levels of education, notably elementary and junior high school. At the time, I thought it difficult and mentally taxing. However, hindsight reveals those educators were teaching me to be a leader. I am forever grateful, and by the time I was in ninth grade, I was leading just about everything in which I took part. My father's preaching took us to Mountain Grove, Missouri, during my freshman year, and I was selected as the Panthers' cheerleading mascot by teachers and administrators who were looking for student leaders. Upon return to Amarillo my sophomore year, I served in several clubs and traveled to many distant states with these groups. I was on the executive leadership team of Student Council in high school, and through that, was qualified to attend the National Leadership Training Center in Estes Park, Colorado, with students from each of the fifty states. Making friends with people from every part of our great country was life-changing for me. I was exposed to some of the best student leaders from each state, and we learned much from each other.

I share with you all these times from my life because I want to emphasize that while I had experienced two horrific attacks, I continued to lead a healthy life by anybody's standards.

Escorted Through Full Disclosure

Early in our married life, Mike announced he and the band were going to stop playing so many engagements, and my heart rejoiced. Although he would continue to be gone most weekends, he would be home a bit more. Being home more regularly on weekends also meant Mike would be available to attend church more often. After about a year of playing the more limited venues, during our fifth year of marriage, Mike became conflicted about how he was using his musical gifts and skills. While he knew the band was playing at venues with a better atmosphere, he was equally convinced he still was not being a good steward of his talents. Subsequently, he began playing more often at church. Eventually, Mike left the weekend dance band scene altogether and became a member of the church's worship team.

Mike's decision about *his* life changed *my* life. I would no longer be spending every weekend alone as a "band widow." From this time forward, I would have the joy of the company of my husband every weekend.

By our twelfth wedding anniversary we had our daughter and son and were in the throes of school plays, PTA, music programs, sports, and the children's activities through our church. One afternoon, while the children were with their grandparents, Mike and I were spending the day running errands.

We drove down a familiar street toward our house, enjoying the beauty of a warm and sunny day. The fresh breeze floated through the open windows in the cab of the pickup. Suddenly, whirling gusts ripped though, scattering grit and propelling a downpour of memories of the childhood episodes I had experienced. Memories of the crimes perpetrated against me had eluded me for many years. With that flood of memories, the convicting revelation of the Holy Spirit disclosed my need to share *the secret* with Mike. Arguing in my mind with the Holy Spirit, I directed to Him the thought, *Lord, I have never told anyone about that. I cannot tell Mike about it.*

My resistance was futile. The Holy Spirit does not retreat. Finally, I succumbed to His bidding and spoke aloud. "Mike, I need to tell you something."

I must have sounded seriously somber, because, with troubled brow and curiously ascending tone, Mike replied, "Okay."

I recounted those childhood incidents as he listened intently. As I disclosed the darkness from my early years, my mouth was dry, my voice shook with nervousness, and an overwhelming sense of shame flooded my heart. I told Mike about the molestation, I described in vivid detail the recurring nightmares which plagued my sleep throughout my childhood. I gave a thorough account of being accosted, the accompanying fear of the moment, escaping the kidnapping, and the subsequent fear I continued to experience after those incidents. As quickly as the nervousness swallowed me as I uttered the first word, an astounding sense of freedom swept through me immediately following the last word.

Mike's response was an expression of sorrow that I had experienced such terrible things at the hands of two men—one who had been part of our family's circle in that tiny Texas town, the other a stranger. Mike's response was the exact one the moment demanded.

You see, I did not need Mike to fix anything. It is not necessary to go back to past events and draw others—those in your present—into those past experiences. Telling someone about an occurrence can bring healing. However, relating an experience to appeal to another's emotions so they will choose an allegiance to you and against another person or group, is manipulative. Because of the Holy Spirit's prompting, disclosing to Mike what had happened to me was all I needed to do so that the attack was no longer shrouded in secretive darkness.

Isaiah spoke of the coming Messiah as one who would, "… open eyes that are blind, to free captives from prison, and to release from the dungeon those who sit in darkness" (Isa. 42:7). At the precise moment I revealed the episodes from my past, this precious Lord of mine escorted me out of my dark dungeon to a radiant new world.

Spiritual Awakening from Blind Paralysis

Disclosing my traumatic childhood incidents to Mike was the beginning of the confrontation process in me. The violations were distant, having occurred more than twenty years before speaking about them with Mike. Filling my life with many friends and keeping my calendar packed with creative activities, I was able to hold the uncomfortable memories at bay, rarely allowing them into my conscious thoughts. Simultaneously, I had created a vacuum within myself.

Only a couple of years after I made my revelation to Mike, we bought and moved into another house several miles across town. One Sunday evening, not long after we settled into our new residence, we were on our way home from church. It was about 9:00 p.m. Gearing my thoughts toward morning, I remembered we were out of milk, so I announced we needed to make that purchase. I fully expected Mike to stop at the market about two blocks from our house, where I would run in, buy the milk, and then we would be home lickety-split. However, Mike headed toward the left-turn lane at the light, routing us homeward. I touched his arm and asked, "Did you hear me?" He nodded affirmatively, then said he would get everyone in the house, and I could take the car and get the milk while the kids were getting ready for bed.

Suddenly, I was overtaken with anxiety. My eyes filled with tears, and I quivered, "You don't understand. I am afraid to go."

The staggering anxiety surprised me as much as it did Mike. He gave me a probing look and, to my great relief, said, "It's okay. We'll get the milk."

We got home and put the milk in the refrigerator and the children in bed. As we turned out lights and headed to our room to ready ourselves for bed, I thanked Mike for his attendance at the market, then apologized profusely for my teary outburst. I explained my uncertainty for the reason of my emotion and assured him I would be okay.

Several days passed, and all was well—until about 3:00 a.m. one weeknight. I opened my eyes from a sound slumber to discover pitch blackness. I could hear Mike snoring but could not see anything. Swiftly, an acute awareness of stillness stifled my breathing. It was impossible to move my arms or legs. It wasn't numbness; I simply could not move. I could not see. Panic enveloped and squeezed me like a tight shoe.

I mouthed, "Mike." My lips opened. No sound came out. My panic grew. I continued trying to get Mike's attention. Whispers began to escape my lips. "Mike. Mike. Mike. Mike." I said his name repeatedly until my voice was able to produce an insignificant sound. My thoughts were wildly running. Still, I could not see. I garnered enough vocal power to say, "Mike." aloud, and he began to stir. I whispered his name several more times.

Silently praying while trying to awaken Mike, a cognizance of my reality became clear. This paralysis was not the arrival of an abrupt physical ailment. It was a spiritual anomaly. Mike turned his head toward me and said, "What?"

In a weak whisper, I said, "There is something in here."

Startled, Mike rolled a one-eighty. Turning from his right-side to the left, he much more emphatically said, "What?"

With insistent whisper, I repeated, "There is something in here." I added, "I need you to pray, *now*!"

I tried to help him understand I was physically paralyzed and blind. My voice was too weak for him to capture my words. He listened, groggy and trying to seize understanding, but I had awakened him from a sound sleep. While he genuinely did not have a full comprehension of what was happening, Mike began to pray. He prayed for several minutes, and as he did, I felt some freedom in my limbs. Mike ended his prayer.

Still cloaked in sinister darkness, I said, "It is still here. Keep praying."

He did.

Mike was fully awake and by then quite conscious of the spiritual battle occurring. His prayer grew intense and singularly directive. As he vocalized his prayer, I began moving my arms and legs in small measure. Voice still faint, I collected enough breath and strength to pray aloud myself. As we prayed together in agreement, the crushing darkness left.

I could see the pinkish amber light of the streetlamp streaming through the window, across the floor, and bending up the wall. The immobility stopped. The oppression lightened, and my chest rose and lowered as I deeply inhaled and exhaled. Then the paralysis vanished. Completely and instantaneously, it left. I had the full activity of my limbs and said to Mike, "It is gone."

As incredible as it may seem, that was the night I was delivered from a half-lived life—a life which had been blinded and paralyzed by fear.

The attempted kidnapping, coupled with *the secret*, had left me with an unmatched level of fear. While I led a normal life externally, I had moments of unsoundness internally, because when filled with fear, there is no room for peace.

Not Alone

Studying Scripture, I found myself in plenty of good company. I learned I was not the only person who had been paralyzed by fear. First Kings, Chapter 19 gives an account of the prophet, Elijah. This prophet of God, a man of strong character and courage, is found running for his life in utter terror from the unscrupulous Jezebel and Ahab. The most notable ruler of Israel, King David, revealed his crippling fear in Psalm 13 when he spoke of being distraught as he wondered if God was hearing, listening, and willing to answer his prayers. We are told in Chapter 28 of Matthew's account of the gospel that even the disciples who traveled with and experienced first-hand the ministry of Jesus, were fearful when Jesus appeared to them as the resurrected Lord.

I learned that these significant historic figures shared some of the same kinds of fears that I, and many others, experience. More significantly, as I followed their stories—as well as the stories of other biblical characters—I also found hope for healing.

The apostle Paul taught the Philippians that when we entrust ourselves to God in Christ Jesus, we communicate our praise and worship to the Lord, as well as prayerfully make our appeal to Him regarding our needs. In doing so, we relieve ourselves of anxiousness, and in exchange for that anxiety, God delivers peace to us. Paul describes it as a peace that surpasses all human understanding. He wrote,

> The Lord is near. Do not be anxious about anything but in every situation, by prayer and petition, with thanksgiving, present your requests to God. And the peace of God, which transcends all understanding, will guard your hearts and your minds in Christ Jesus. (Phil. 4:5b-7)

In his second letter to Timothy, Paul wrote, "For God has not given us a spirit of fear, but of power and of love and of a sound mind" (2 Tim. 1:7 NKJV). The fear that plagued me was stealing my peace. I desperately longed for this peaceful mind and mighty power in the Lord.

In revealing those traumatic childhood events to Mike, then to a close mentor and friend, I received a lesson of profound importance. When we bring something into the light, it can no longer hold us hostage. That thing—incident, experience, sinful behavior, fear, etc.—is rendered powerless over us, because it is no longer a secret the enemy of our souls can use against us. The enemy can no longer taunt us with, "What if someone finds out?" because we have chosen to bring it into the light and conquer it. God's peace replaces darkness and oppression, and His peace brings with it a sound mind. These Scriptures reveal to us that the laser focus of the light of Christ burns through the iron shackles of anxiety, shame, and fear, illuminating the exquisite beauty of what was once confined.

Glimmers of the Crown

For God has not given us a spirit of fear, but of power and of love and of a sound mind. (1 Tim. 1:7 NKJV)

The Lord is near. Do not be anxious about anything but in every situation, by prayer and petition, with thanksgiving, present your requests to God. And the peace of God, which transcends all understanding, will guard your hearts and your minds in Christ Jesus. (Phil. 4:5b-7 NIV)

CHAPTER 3

The Claim Jumper

In the mining profession, sometimes claim jumpers will try to occupy a mine to which they have no legal claim. Claim jumpers usurp the place of a legal owner by deceit, pushing, manipulating, or bullying them away, to cash-in on the valuable deposits held within the claim.

The claim jumper in my life—the greatest hindrance to my personal and spiritual success—was fear. On the surface, my life appeared normal, yet I was filled with trepidation about everything. The private, domineering fearful thoughts were held deep within, pushing me further and further away from my sense of value, creating an officious lack of confidence. This led to feeling undeserving of virtually all I wanted for myself, as well as things I yearned to pursue in each facet of life—family, work, church, music, leadership, and virtually everything else.

Fool's Gold

Performing was a common occurrence throughout my life, particularly in a church. I began as a singer in a trio with my sister and our mother. I usually sang the lead. My sister could carry a voice part from the time she was young, so she naturally sang alto, and our mother would sing the tenor line. That morphed into my singing harmonies with them, then singing with others. As I grew older, I was asked to bring spoken testimony along with our music.

Because musical performance and theatrical productions were a regular occurrence, I did not give much thought to the idea of being on stage. Conversely, in all the stage work, I did not want to be in the spotlight. I ascribed to a team mentality that when we all give our best effort, the entire production will go well. I also preferred being stage left or right rather than at the center. Thus, I was a paradox in the world of performers. Being on the platform with a group was normal but being in the spotlight was terrifying. While I did not have a drive to be seen and noticed, I wanted assurance that whatever work I presented met the highest standards.

The quiet, perfectionistic, compliant child grew into the same kind of adult. My first professional employment was at a bank working alongside the senior vice president. Because I assisted with projects for the president and the chairman of the board, it was imperative my letters, reports to the board, preparation of commercial loans—as well as my ability to converse with all those people in varying contexts—delivered at an impeccably professional level.

I approached every segment of my life in the same way. I wanted to be the perfect employee, anticipating the need before it arose, and supplying the most excellent and aesthetically pleasing reports ever typed. At home, I wanted to be the perfect wife—the one with a perfectly clean house and perfectly planned meals. The laundry hamper should be consistently empty with every item washed, dried, ironed, folded, and placed where it belongs. Each car should be filled with fuel, in perfect working order, and ready for the road at a moment's notice.

Perfection at every level was my aim, and achieving it was my game. I thought *everything* was my responsibility and was troubled by the notion of not getting it all done. If I did not meet this wildly disproportionate standard of my own making, I believed I would not be accepted as I wanted. Without achieving this standard, I knew my supervisor, my peers, my husband, his parents, and their entire family would think I was a deadbeat. I could not risk that. Nor could I gamble with even the idea of disappointing my parents. Perfectionism is fear on steroids.

The Treacherous Work of Fear

Fear is one of the highest walls we must climb and one of the most difficult to scale. I dare say there is likely not a human being on this planet who does not have at least one wall of some fear to climb.

Fear originates from a variety of sources. Some people are fearful of the future and the unknown; maybe they are dealing with an illness or financial struggles. Some people conjure up all the "what ifs" for every situation, and their lives riddled with worry. Others are fearful of the past—maybe early years of indiscretion could be revealed, or they are running from events perpetrated upon them. Fear can be incited in us presently because of past circumstances that were embarrassing or discouraging to our confidence. For instance, let's say my company is planning a big project, and I am a key player on the team that puts the plan together. All the brainstorming takes place, and we construct a plan. It is time to present the idea, and my employer actively listens to my presentation. However, their response makes me cringe as they shred my presentation with a lack of enthusiasm, negative observations, and criticism of my ideas. With each comment, my confidence shrinks.

With that kind of experience, I might be apprehensive about making another presentation to my employer in the future. Not only that, if those thoughts take over, my ability to function as a decision-maker at every level could be affected.

Perfectionism is fear on steroids. Perfectionism is the fool's gold of fear masked as confidence and competence.

Fear manifested itself in my life in several ways. I was comfortable being fun and silly with my friends. Still, lurking in my mind was the dread that others might think me unintelligent or that someone might disagree with me and force me to defend my thoughts. Would I be able to put the words together to explain my thinking? Would I flub it all and say something unintelligible?

When and where did all this fear begin? How did I become so filled with fear?

Fear began its deceitful work in me through the gateway of being sexually molested as a young child. It continued its work with the attempted kidnapping and later, through other, less traumatic circumstances.

When I was a sophomore in high school, our small, quiet city made national headlines due to the brutal murder of a young mother. The perpetrator was unknown, and therefore our entire area was on high alert.

One evening, while authorities were in the throes of the all-points search for the murderer, I found myself fortunate to be off work early. I was home with no plans. My friends were working. My sister no longer lived at home, and the rest of our family was out for a dinner event. Intolerably bored, I turned on the television while hoping for something better to do.

A light rain began and quickly became a downpour. The overcast sky grew darker as the sun set, and a thunderstorm intensified. I watched through the picture window of our living room as the lightning silhouetted the billowing clouds. The thunder crashed and reached a crescendo with the approaching storm. I turned to watch television, and the crackling boom of an unnervingly close lightning bolt jolted me to my feet. Everything in the house went dark—no television, no lights, no streetlights, no clock on the oven. There was nothing, just smothering darkness.

My heart began to pound. I was terrified. Was this indeed because of the lightning, or was the murderer on the lam, now at my house? Was he aware I was alone? Was he lurking in the darkness just outside the front door? These thoughts became more plausible to me, although they also grew increasingly like a subpar, B-movie plot.

Groping through the darkness and hoping my eyes would quickly adjust to the dimness of the tiny sliver of moon glowing through the large picture window, I found the drawer that held the flashlight. The batteries were good, and it switched on, but it only provided a narrow beam of light. I made my way back to the living room and set the flashlight on the coffee table, hoping to light the room. Quaking visibly, I hunkered into a spot on the couch, flashlight within arm's reach. The rest of the house seemed to grow blacker with each moment of silent darkness.

The minutes trudged by with the speed of a sloth. As I sat, wide-eyed, curled into as small a crouch as possible in my couch corner, trying to see down the hallway, the silence fractured with shrieks of an alarm clock. Lights flickered in the kitchen, and the living room lamps blinked.

A power company crew quickly responded and reset the neighborhood transformer rendered powerless by lightning. All the house lights returned to normal. Still shuddering, I walked quickly and carefully to the bedroom to hush the terrorizing clock. The glow of streetlamps returned, and I could see there were no human shadows on the front porch.

How quickly an ordinary situation became extraordinary and redirected my thoughts to the dread of illusory evils. My mind abruptly shifted from finding a way to enjoy a night off work to fear-filled imaginations that were not only unrealistic but created added elements of fear. Through my anxiety and improbable worries, it never occurred to me that Freckles, our beagle, was not making a sound. Had anyone been near our house, or even near our yard, Freckles would have howled and barked until either the threat to his territory was gone or someone went outside to quiet him. Freckles rested calmly sheltered inside his doghouse. The only noise outside was the howling wind and occasional claps of thunder; the only movement inside was when I adjusted my shaking legs or moved the flashlight. Every nanosecond of terror occurred in the confines of my mind. This constant companion of foreboding was not one I wished to keep.

Enemies Unseen

In his letters to the churches in Rome, Corinth, and Ephesus, the apostle Paul wrote that our enemy is not carnal, meaning not of flesh and blood. Instead, our enemy is spirit. Our enemy is what Paul refers to as the principalities and powers of darkness that war against our souls. Paul described it this way because the archenemy of humanity is the fallen angel, Lucifer, whom we refer to as Satan. Along with his minions—those angels we call demons, who were cast from Heaven along with him—Satan is at work to destroy us. They do their work from the inside, within our spirit.

Beginnings awaken our spirit to the Holy Spirit to confront issues that hinder our success.

Because our enemy is of the spiritual realm, our weapons to defend ourselves are also of spirit. (This concept will be addressed in greater detail in Chapter 9.) Paul compares our spiritual weaponry to that of the armor of warfare on the battlefield. Paul's imagery affords the reader a full understanding that God equips us with what is needed to win the war for our souls. Paul describes the armor and weaponry in Ephesians 6:10-18. Each piece is for protection in defense of arrows that come at us, with one exception. The one piece of equipment we have for offensive tactics is the sword of the spirit, which is the word of God.

The understood message in Paul's writing is that we will face many battles. Jesus taught that we would experience trials and troublesome times. John recorded in his gospel an account of Jesus speaking of the enemy of our souls, where He said the focus of the enemy is, "to steal and kill and destroy" (John 10:10).

Satan calculates the way he does his work because destruction is his end goal. He uses many deceitful tactics to steal from us, kill our spirits, and bring about our destruction from within by taking our peace and creating confusion. Waging battles relentlessly, he attacks from every angle to carry out his mission. As you can see, hurled at me over and again were the fiery arrows of fear. Sheathed in the proper armor is the only way to deflect Satan's ammunition.

Jesus completed His statement in John 10:10 by saying that He (Jesus) came to bring life, abundant life. It is time for us to brandish the sword of the spirit as our guide to connecting to this abundant life in Jesus. Let us examine our lives in the light of the Word and find and confront where Satan is at work to destroy our success. As we progress, we will uncover the plan and purpose for which God has designed us and start walking in it.

PART 1: CONFRONT

Glimmers of the Crown

You are from God, little children, and have overcome them; because greater is He who is in you than he who is in the world. (1 John 4:4 NASB)

For God is *not* the author of confusion but of peace, as in all the churches of the saints. (1 Cor. 14:33 NKJV, author's emphasis)

PART 2

Collapse

Shake off your dust;
rise up ...
Free yourself
from the chains on your neck

CHAPTER 4

From Stone to Slabs—Step Out of Your Chains

From the crown to the pavilion of a gemstone, eight areas can be faceted to reveal the brilliance of the stone. These surfaces are carefully sliced in fragments to reveal the crystallized beauty under the rough edges. Similarly, we must allow the faceting process to occur within ourselves. There is a cutting away of the old to reveal the loveliness of the jewels contained within us. Our Creator has entrusted us with gifts from Himself in a rainbow of colors. Cutting away from us the old and rough unveils the clarity and brilliance of these jewels. As we bevel off the unnecessary baggage of the past, the light of truth shines through to bring forward God's purpose in us.

Take Off the Old Way of Living

In our re-awakening to the Holy Spirit, we have identified the problem causing our anguish. The issue may be something perpetrated against us. It may be something created from our reckless actions. The underlying matter could also be unaddressed, unconfessed, and willful rebellion against God's precepts and ordinances. In simpler terms, the predominant obstruction barring us from succeeding in life could be an unconfessed sin. Our issues may be a combination of any, or all, these things. Whatever the case, the matter creates a barrier prohibiting us from realizing abundant life in Christ, which, in turn, affects every area of life. When we have identified and confronted the current issue, we can move to the next step: COLLAPSE the problem and rid ourselves of it.

Verse 2 of the Isaiah 52 passage instructs, "Shake off your dust; rise up…Free yourself from the chains on your neck, daughter of Zion, now a captive."

This instructional statement clarifies two things. First, our daughter of Zion has a problem. She is in captivity. Second, Isaiah gives her the secret to finding her freedom. I dare say she may have been surprised to learn how clearly defined the line to her liberation was. The way for our captive daughter to become free is to loosen her chains and remove them.

Wait. What? Yes, you read that correctly. Isaiah gave the directive—not to the jailer, but the imprisoned woman.

When we identify the obstacle to our progress, the responsibility to COLLAPSE and remove it belongs to us. Let me reassert: *the responsibility is ours.* We know from experience the obstacle will not remove itself, and no one else has the ability, power, or authority to remove it from us. Even the Lord is not going to sweep in and brush it away without our choosing to separate ourselves from the problematic issue.

In this portion of our Scripture passage, Isaiah coaches us with three directives. When Scripture gives an instruction, carried within that is the understanding we are also given the authority to follow it. To enable us to savor and digest the instruction given to this imprisoned daughter, and to apply it to our present situation, we will break it into smaller, bite-sized morsels.

Shake It Off

The image in this passage is of a woman, captured against her will. Held as a prisoner, she is clad in shackles and chains. She is seated on the floor of a prison cell. Her countenance is fallen. Her gaze is expressionless as her eyes roam the floor, and she sees only her disheveled condition. Our daughter cannot bear the sound of metal scratching and clanging, so she sits silently. Dust collects around her exhausted, feeble body. She has given up on being released from captivity. She stays on the ground, seated on the earth.

A Little Housekeeping

I have lived most of my life in Amarillo, Texas. Amarillo is in the center of the "crown" of Texas, also known as the panhandle. Each year, Amarillo receives the distinction of being ranked one of the top ten windiest cities in the world, for both consistency and velocity. Often, the city ranks in the top five in this wind category. With that, Amarillo is also hailed the windiest city in the United States.[3] (Sorry to disappoint those who may have thought Chicago held this distinction.) Breezes sway the grassy plains at an average of 13.6 mph, and often, gusts burst through at twice that speed or more. Amarillo's semi-arid climate receives wind and rainfall from the south during the spring and summer, while fall and winter bring northwesterly winds and snow from the mountains of Colorado and northern New Mexico. I share this weather pattern information with you to help you understand that Amarillo's climate is dry, windy, and dusty most of the time.

If you clean your home in Amarillo at least once a week, the dust does not have time to settle and collect. However, if you postpone cleaning, the dust accumulates, begins piling on top of itself, and creates a visible layer. If you have ever had the opportunity to clean out a garage, cellar, attic, or basement, you have seen accumulated dust.

I remember my Granny's little storage room at her house in southeastern Oklahoma. In it were some of the most delectable culinary delights—vegetables canned fresh from her garden, honey with the comb from the hive, and homemade preserves, jams, and jellies. It was a delight when she would break out a fresh jar of homemade goodness. Yum!

However, as a young child, I did not like to be the one who had to select the jar from the storage room. You see, my grandparents retired on a five-acre tract located on a rural route, and they lived in an old, farmhouse. It was a cozy, two-bedroom house, heated by a wood burning stove and cooled with an evaporative cooler. A room added to the back of the house, adjacent the bathroom, provided space expressly for storage. There was no insulation or special wall treatment. It was merely a shell to protect its contents from the elements.

In that room was an extra bed to accommodate an abundance of guests (namely, my sister and me), and underneath that bed were the jars, packed in box pallets. Along with the jars were spiders and their webs, other creepy crawlies, and several layers of dust. When sent to gather a new container, I would slowly unlock the hook and eye latch, and with great trepidation, open the storage room door. Once inside, I would bend down, close my eyes, reach under the bed, and quickly yank out a box. Seconds later, eyes open, I would read the tops of the jars, select one, and shove the pallet back under the bed. Jar in hand, I would shake it sideways so the dust would puff up and fall to the floor. Then I would wipe the jar with my hand, lock the room, and carry the prize to the kitchen. It was quite a process.

One thing we can be sure of is that when we are told to "shake off your dust" (just as I did with Granny's canned goods), we know the dust has been collecting for some time.

Like the jar under the bed, the daughter of Zion in our Scripture has been seated in her position for an extended period. The dust has been collecting around her. The portrait our Scripture paints is that of a woman who cannot see past her circumstance. Our daughter of Zion locked her focus on the problem at hand and wallowed in it.

Like the daughter in this passage, when we experience some significant difficulty or tragedy in life, we can allow that situation to rule and reign in our thoughts. As those become our leading thoughts, they pull us into whatever action—or inaction—we take. Overtaken with those ruminations and subsequent activity, before we realize it, we become comfortable in our dysfunction. For example, it has been documented by experts in the fields of sociology and psychology that people who grow up in homes where domestic violence is prevalent tend to enter other abusive relationships. The cycle of abuse is what they know to be normal. So, their dysfunction becomes their norm, and consequently, befalls the next generation, resulting in intergenerational dysfunction.[4]

Sometimes our dysfunction is less evident to the outside observer. In my case, although fear filled my soul, the people around me were unaware of my inner turmoil. Nevertheless, I had become accustomed to my dysfunction, observing and participating in life through the lens of fear.

Isaiah teaches that this operative dysfunction does not have to be a lifelong sentence. While we filter everything through our life experiences, we do not have to allow our negative experiences to cloud our present or taint our future. For me, I realized I did not want to dwell with this overpowering distress any longer. It had seized control of every detail of my life for many years. I was tired of it. I was ready to shake off the dust of fear. I needed to COLLAPSE it for all time.

The problem of fear in my life was magnified because I focused on the fear itself, or the things of which I was afraid. When we magnify something, that means we make it appear larger than it is. When you hold a magnifying glass to a printed page, the words appear larger, so they are easier to read. The print on the page does not enlarge; nonetheless, the curved glass augments its appearance.

Comparably, on the opposite end of the spectrum, when you look into a side mirror on a vehicle, there are eight words etched on it: *Objects in mirror are closer than they appear.* The mirror conveys the message, with each use, that it is designed to *distort* the appearance of the objects.

In both cases, the actual object does not change; only its appearance is distorted to enlarge or reduce.

Similarly, the lens of fear was distorting the image in my mind. The Lord was showing me through this Scripture, that I had focused my attention on fear and dread, magnifying them in my heart and soul, and making me fearful. Fearful is defined as *full of fear*.

On the other hand, the reason the side mirror on a vehicle distorts the image by shrinking objects is to reveal the whole picture. By seeing the entire scene, the driver is less likely to back into something a full-sized image may not allow him or her to see. It pulls the whole picture together into a smaller area, bringing the world into view so that it can be safely navigated.

Magnifying fear caused me to reduce the reality of my whole life, provoking me to feel less valuable, less worthy, and less able to offer anything of significance to the world around me.

In this step of the process, we COLLAPSE our challenging nemesis. We do so by first seeing its role and function—or more accurately, its dysfunction—in our lives. Then, we bring the perplexing antagonist into its proportionate perspective in respect to the entire scene of our lives. From this vantage point, we are enabled to trigger its collapse.

To COLLAPSE means to break down or crumble from within, suddenly. The word *suddenly* is significant in this process. Although this opponent to our success has been challenging us for quite some time, when we choose to bid farewell to it, it will seem sudden. It will initially be painful to separate from it. As we move away from it, we will watch it become smaller, less significant, less useful, and less valuable. We will watch as it *suddenly* crumbles into oblivion. We will begin to feel victorious.

When a problem has presented throughout our lives, we must stop its damaging effects. We collapse such negative issues by breaking down these hindrances to our success, shrinking their appearance, reducing their effectiveness, and ridding ourselves of them, permanently.

Rise Up

Breaking down fear was the one thing I needed to do, but how could I accomplish it? The answer is in our Scripture. The second instruction is to *rise up*.

To rise up indicates preparing to act. To shake off the dust and find freedom, our prisoner cannot remain seated. She must rise up to be ready for action. If we are to rid ourselves of self-limiting beliefs and success-prohibiting issues, we cannot stay in the same place we have been. Instead, we must move. The way to cast off fully the things that bind our hearts is to stand up, shake them loose from head to toe, and remove them.

When we bring our flaws and frailties into the light, they can no longer hold us hostage.

Just as a cloud puffed up when the literal dust was shaken off my Granny's jars of canned goods, a figurative cloud will puff up in our minds when we rise and disturb the comfort of our dysfunction. As we progress through this dusting off process, we realize quickly that disturbing the dust of dysfunction can be unsettling. This cloud contains the particles of our problems, and if we are not mindful, we can choke on the debris as it swirls and blows back in an attempt to settle into its usual, hollowed-out space. However, intentionally stirring up the powder of aged troubles reveals that those dark specks were concealing the mine of our well-being. Like claim jumpers, these issues stake an illegal claim to the mine and strip it of its intrinsic value by eroding the jewels of joy and peace, as well as the personal success of being all we are created to be and fulfilling our place in God's Kingdom. Rising up, we find ourselves filled with a greater desire to protect our hearts from that resettling than allowing it to fall back into its old space. Our spirit is more determined to rid ourselves entirely of the undignified dust of the past.

In my case, I began moving the dust of fearfulness by consciously making a mental note of things which brought on any level of fear—from mild intimidation to full-on terror. Then, I began to require myself to face those things head-on, to stand firm against fear, carrying out things I previously would have been terrified to do. Remember, I was afraid of everything that required any amount of attention be on me—particularly if I would be the central focus in any way. I knew the struggle during a face-off with fear would be enormous.

The showdown officially began when a respected Bible teacher asked me to fill his spot while he was absent due to an extended vacation. I was honored to be asked by someone so revered and admired for his teaching skill and personal integrity, as well as a man who had become a valued friend. Before I gave myself time to think it through, I agreed to teach in his stead.

By the time class date arrived, I was a nervous wreck. The class began at 9:30 a.m., and I was expected to teach for about forty-five minutes of the sixty-minute class time. It was late summer, and I wore a white, cap-sleeved suit, with a deep V-neck, and gold buttons. As I began the introduction, I could feel the heat rise from my core into my neck and face. We were in an un-airconditioned, second-floor room, filled with about sixty adults. I opened the lesson with prayer and began teaching.

I looked across the crowded room and made eye contact with those who seemed sympathetic. As perspiration made way to the surface of my forearms, I felt my hands become clammy, and my heart pounded out a cadence that seemed to echo in my head. Thoughts in my synapses were screaming *Check your buttons. Check your collar. Check your skirt. Check your collar. Check your watch. Check your collar. Check your notes. Check your collar. No one's listening. Check your collar.*

To my relief, I completed the lesson, and class ended. I gathered my note cards and Bible and made my way to the back of the room for a gulp of cool water and a breath of fresh air.

Standing there waiting was my dear friend, Sandy, who said, "You did a wonderful job, Leah." With sparkling blue eyes and pearly white grin, she added playfully, "By the way, your collar is fine." Every time I had the thought to check my collar, my had carried out that command like an involuntary reflex.

That first experience of standing up against my arch enemy, which was fear, armed with every ounce of grit and determination I could muster, was a thrilling victory.

The woman in our Scripture is poised to encounter that same kind of victory. Isaiah depicts this daughter of Zion as a prisoner. She is captive. She is chained. However, there is something unusual about her captivity. She is chained only by the neck. Her hands and feet are free.

Many chains can bind our lives. Fear bound me tightly. Others are chained by strongholds such as anger, bitterness, resentment, grief, pain, a foul mouth, unforgiveness, a critical spirit, jealousy, gossip, and a host of other issues of the heart and mind. No matter the name on the chain, when linked to these issues, they steal our breath, and we choke and suffocate our success in life.

The prisoner in Isaiah's account is instructed to loosen her chains. Like her, we are free to reach up with our dirty hands, take hold of the collars, release the pins, and remove the chains. We hold the key—the key of free will. With the ability to choose, we carry the responsibility of bearing the consequences of our choices. Even when our issues originate from having been subjected to someone else's actions against us, we must take ownership of how we hold on to them. We can choose to be free from the chains that bind us. We must loosen these chains from our necks to stop obstructing our ability to breathe, to function at full power, and to succeed at being all God created us to be.

Breathing Fresh Air

For the sake of helping us fully understand this concept of collapsing our success-prohibiting issues, let me suggest another analogy. Many years ago, we used roll-away beds for sleep-over company. They were one step better than a cot—they were metal bed frames with fully exposed metal springs, legs on rollers, and a lumpy rectangle thinly disguised as a mattress. They folded in half for storage but were quite bulky, so people usually kept their roll-away in a storage building or garage. When pulled out for use, roll-away beds often smelled like mothballs wrapped in the musty dust of the storage building, and they were uncomfortable.

Today, the extra bedding dilemma has been helped with the design of deep-pocket air mattresses. We can pull an air mattress from a closet shelf, inflate it, and put on the floor of just about any room for additional sleep-over company. Designed with individual chambers, an air mattress is inflated, then plugged to retain the air. After its use, the bed is prepared for storage by emptying all the air chambers. With the valve opened, the mattress is pressed from the farthest end of the chambers, forcing the air out through the opening. Flattening the mattress allows it to be folded and stored in a small space, unlike a musty, bulky, roll-away bed. More significantly, the air mattress is prepared for its next use, to be re-inflated with fresh, new air.

In our minds, we administer the same process. Our brains have chambers where we have tucked away incidents, experiences, memories, significant, and insignificant, life events. We harbor things such as fear, detrimental experiences, hurt, and pain. When we're ready to rid ourselves of this negative thought pattern, we choose to press that thing (in my case, fear) out of the chambers of our mind. Simultaneously, we are preparing those chambers for something new. We can refill our mind's chambers with positive, God-honoring things, such as faith and trust in Him.

The entire concept of collapsing our negative mindsets centers on the axis of our thought life. It is entirely about what happens in our minds. Our thoughts govern our actions. We become the way we think. Thus, it is imperative that our thoughts lead us in a direction we desire to go. Dr. Caroline Leaf, a researcher in the study of the human brain, wrote in her book, *Switch on Your Brain*, "As we think, we change the physical nature of our brain. As we consciously direct our thinking, we can wire out toxic patterns of thinking and replace them with healthy thoughts."[5]

Thought Life

Not all our thoughts originate with us. We need to understand; the enemy of our souls tempts us with ideas. It is not a sin to have thoughts; it is what we do with those thoughts that determines the outcome. The reason we know thoughts themselves are not sins is that the allure Satan used with Jesus was temptation with thoughts. Jesus was indeed tempted—yet, the Bible also says Jesus was without sin.

In the fourth chapter of Matthew's Gospel, he wrote of the account of Jesus enduring and overcoming Satan's temptation. Jesus was on a forty day fast. He was hungry, and Satan knew it. The thought of turning the stone to bread occurred to Jesus because Satan taunted Jesus with the *idea* through the avenue of his hungry stomach. Jesus had hidden the Word in His heart, like precious jewels in a treasure chest. So, when He experienced the force of temptation, He refuted and squelched it by quoting Scripture to Satan. "It is written: 'Man shall not live on bread alone, but on every word that comes from the mouth of God'" (Matt. 4:4).

Satan tempted Jesus with ideas of using ungodly ways to fulfill His hunger, inappropriate use of His power and authority, and the prideful rule of the kingdoms of earth. Jesus, through His experience with temptation, taught us we could overcome the temptation to sin, no matter the kind— lust of the flesh, pride of life, etc. In the Gospel account of these temptations, Jesus is portrayed as having a conversation with the tempter. Jesus, being both God and man, was able to converse with Satan face-to-face. We are tempted in our spirit only, not with a face-to-face encounter. In each instance of temptation, Jesus was able to withstand the seedbed of thoughts hurled into His mind because He recognized the identity of their origin; He shows us we should scrutinize our thoughts in the same way. Jesus confronted the tempting thoughts for what they were, teaching us we can also valiantly face and overcome temptation. He collapsed each temptation with correct thoughts about Himself and His identity in God and with correct thoughts about the issue at hand from the Word of God. Jesus gave us the formula for overcoming temptation.

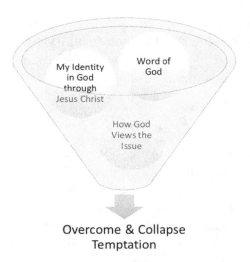

Overcome & Collapse
Temptation

The good news for us is that, like Jesus, we can choose the things about which we meditate. In his letter to the church at Corinth, Paul taught, "We are destroying speculations, and every lofty thing raised up against the knowledge of God, and we are taking every thought captive to the obedience of Christ" (2 Cor. 10:5 NASB). In the same way, Jesus showed us through His experience with His thought life that we have the authority to stop thoughts in their tracks and bring them into obedience to Christ and what He would have us think.

> *When we can identify the source of our pain, we can rid ourselves of the symptoms of that pain.*

In my case, as perhaps it is in your life, crimes were committed against me. Through those crimes, Satan stole from my childhood the ability to be carefree. He stole my innocence. He took my sense of value. He tried to destroy me with shame and feelings of inadequacy, and he tried to kill my spirit.

Outside of illness, our pain is often brought on by sins—ours or the sin of another perpetrated upon us. When we can identify the source of our pain, we can rid ourselves of the symptoms of that pain. The incident or situation that brought the pain is not necessarily gone from our minds because it stays stored within our memory, but it is rendered useless, ineffective, and powerless to debilitate us. We have COLLAPSED our trauma.

Hostages of Unforgiveness

With the subject of collapsing our hindrances to success, we must address forgiveness. We cannot hold someone else hostage over our issues. Though the problem or issue we are dealing with may have been instigated by or through another person, we cannot fix other people—just as I cannot go back and erase the long-ago crimes against me. We can only fix ourselves.

Forgiveness. I must forgive.

In Chapter 15 of the Gospel of John is the account of Jesus speaking of Himself as the Vine. He states that He is the Vine, and we, those who believe in Him and place their trust in Him, are branches of that Vine. There is a Vine Dresser, who is God, and He prunes the branches of the Vine. In light of this Scripture, I would like to explore the concept of pruning.

Pruning rids a stalk or trunk of unnecessary and unproductive growth. These growths started well, then died away, or are extensions from a part of the vine or trunk previously pruned. The dead growths dry out, become discolored and unsightly, and create an obstruction to the healthy growth. Sucker branches are living, unproductive growths on the trunk brought about by stressful conditions. Sucker branches detract from the beauty of the plant because they often look different from the rest of the plant, and because they are fully alive, they hamper and suck the life away from the wanted, healthy growth. In either case, these dead or sucker branches must be selectively removed.

Correlating Jesus' analogy of the Vine Dresser's pruning to our lives today, we can conclude that we have unhealthy things in our lives that are hampering our growth and success and need to be pruned. For three years, Jesus lived life with His disciples and taught them face-to-face. Together, they encountered various people and their situations. In our time, Jesus walks this life with us through His spiritual presence, the Holy Spirit (John 14:15-27). Because of this, we understand Jesus is talking about the Holy Spirit revelation. Though his Holy Spirit, the Lord reveals to us those things in our hearts and lives that are unnecessary, unproductive, and even things that are spiritually dead (also called dead work). Any combination of these extraneous growths being active in our lives obstructs the relationship between the Lord and us. This spiritual upheaval within us, consequently, affects our interpersonal relationships and success in every other area of life. The things we carry around—exaggerated fear, unforgiveness, bitterness, anger, resentment, and the many other harmful things we can store in our hearts—are all dead work. The Lord reveals those dead things to us for the express purpose of pruning. He shows us what needs to be cut out of our hearts, detached from us completely, and removed from our lives.

Often, we will allow and endure the cutting away of dead work, and shortly afterward we reattach it to ourselves because we harbor unforgiveness. When we choose not to forgive another, we are attaching a dead branch to ourselves. Immediately, without realizing it, we begin breathing our precious life into that dead branch.

Withholding forgiveness is dead work. Consequently, it brings death to relationships. The lack of forgiveness we may hold so dearly because we believe we have earned the right to have it is holding us hostage in its death grip.

Picture a logging chain clinched around a huge tree. Unforgiveness is like a large branch attached to us with a heavy chain that, as we drag it around, can choke the life out of us. We hear the name of the person we are withholding forgiveness from, and we cringe. We see them out somewhere, and we bristle. We see their picture or that of someone close to them, and it affects us. In any of these instances, we redirect our thoughts toward our anger, resentment, and bitterness, and a physical response follows—rapid heart rate, increased blood pressure, perspiration, tensed muscles, furrowed brow, tightened hands, clenched teeth, a quicker pace, and a plethora of other physical responses. It not only affects our emotions, it affects us physically. Ultimately, our spirit and spiritual walk are negatively affected.

There is an oft-referenced adage which states that forgiveness is not for the offender as much as it is for the offended. While there is a measure of truth in this, there is a more sobering reality about forgiveness versus unforgiveness. Matthew quotes Jesus as saying, "For if you forgive other people when they sin against you, your heavenly Father will also forgive you. *But if you do not forgive* others their sins, *your Father will not forgive* your sins.*" (Matt. 6:14-15 (author's emphasis)).

Jesus taught, with no uncertainty, that God is not pleased with us when we harbor unforgiveness. He warned and counseled us regarding the consequences of our choosing not to forgive others of their wrongdoing against us. The need to forgive is not up for debate. Our unforgiveness toward others results in God choosing not to forgive us. Jesus' words are difficult to receive because they feel abrasive when we read and grasp their gravity. We readily accept verse fourteen in Matthew's account (Matt. 6), when Jesus speaks of God's forgiveness toward us when we are mercifully forgiving toward others. Still, we must take the whole teaching, allowing the entire spiritual truth of it. We cannot accept the parts we like and reject what does not make us feel happy.

Unforgiveness is like those items in our closet we cannot bear to relinquish. We keep holding onto them, emotionally attached to the memory of receiving them or thinking one day they will fit or be useful. They keep hanging there, unused. We cannot put new apparel in the closet because the old, unworkable pieces we refuse to surrender are still there, taking up valuable space.

The problem with unforgiveness and other negative heart attitudes is they corrupt every other facet of life. Think about the people you know. Have you ever been around a person who has a critical spirit? I am talking about a person who finds the negative side of every issue. It seems to be a natural outgrowth of who they are.

I know people like this, and it is disheartening to be around them. They put a damper on every positive thing. Every compliment contains a caveat. For every good thing that happens, they contribute an adverse comment.

The chances are high that such people did not start life with this attitude. They, like everyone on the planet, had some negative things that occurred in their life. Rather than allowing it to roll of their backs and away from them, they absorbed it all, tucked it away, and chose to carry it everywhere. It is a constant source of ready ammunition for them. What I have found is that people with this critical bent do not realize how much of an energy drain their negativity is to the people around them.

We must surrender unforgiveness and all other negative heart attitudes as God reveals them to us. God does not show these issues to us to hurt or condemn us. He reveals them to us so we can surrender them to His authority, and He can grow us in His grace. Paul taught the Ephesians to leave behind the way they previously lived and thought when he wrote, "In reference to your former manner of life, you lay aside the old self, which is being corrupted in accordance with the lusts of deceit" (Eph. 4:22 NASB).

When we surrender ourselves and lay aside our former way of thinking, giving ourselves without reservation entirely to the Lord, we will find we have the power and authority to shake off the dust of wrong understanding of who we are. We can rise up knowing our problems and circumstances do not have the right to destroy us. We can ready ourselves and remove the chains that bind us to the prison walls. We tear down the walls of our prison and collapse wrong thinking. When those walls begin to fall, we know we have made room in our hearts and minds to bring in a new thing.

Glimmers of the Crown

But I say, walk habitually in the [Holy] Spirit [seek Him and be responsive to His guidance], and then you will certainly not carry out the desire of the sinful nature [which responds impulsively without regard for God and His precepts]. For the sinful nature has its desire which is opposed to the Spirit, and the [desire of the] Spirit opposes the sinful nature; for these [two, the sinful nature and the Spirit] are in direct opposition to each other [continually in conflict], so that you [as believers] do not [always] do whatever [good things] you want to do. ... If we [claim to] live by the [Holy] Spirit, we must also walk by the Spirit [with personal integrity, godly character, and moral courage—our conduct empowered by the Holy Spirit]. (Gal. 5:16-17, 25 AMP)

PART 3

Collect

Clothe yourself with strength
Put on your garments of splendor

CHAPTER 5

Prisms of Color — Create the Facets

Effervescence from Friction

On our journey from the deep caverns, we tunneled through the deposits to probe and mine the valuable vein of gemstones which form our God-ordained purpose. When the Lord, our Lapidary, uncovers the gem by removing the rough from our outer edges, it is only the first part of the process. We feel the surgically precise incisions as the Artisan saws our solid stone into smaller, workable slabs. We endure the vibration as He grinds us down into our rough form, an identifiable shape like a preformed stone. With supreme gracefulness, He cools us with the life-giving water of His Spirit, while simultaneously, He sands us with the most delicate of control. Over and again, He applies sand, friction, and water, removing the deep, intricate, and obscure scratches. This process reveals the emerging splendor of the gem that is our life.

Collection of Finery

What do we do with the information we have acquired thus far? We have found the source of anguish which has pilfered tremendous measures of time and energy from our lives, stunting our ability to progress toward the ultimate vision of spiritual and personal success. We looked this lifelong foe in the eye. We told this fiendish brute we would no longer allow it to terrorize us. We told the malevolent ogre we would no longer be attached to it or associated with it, in any way. We stood up and shook it loose from ourselves. Then, we walked away from it and sent it packing in the other direction with orders never to trouble us again.

Like the rough stone picked from the rocky wall of a mine, carted up the shaft, and out into the light of day, we have trekked far on this journey. We have spiraled through shackles and turned the key, unlocking the pins of heavy chains engraved with monikers of past events, hurtful moments, and personal failures. We slogged our way through the filth of the behavior of others toward us, setting our focus and gritting through as we emerged from the dusty dungeon. We are now standing just outside the shadows of that dark, gloomy prison. We have reached the halfway point.

Halfway is an extraordinary place to be. We assess what lies behind and the possibilities awaiting ahead. Are we willing to continue? Will we submit and suffer the growing pains of change, then reap the rewards of that growth? Or will we experience the pain, stagnation, and loss, of remaining the same?

Halfway. We can call it the crisis point. Halfway is the intersection at which we make a life-altering decision to stop or go. We can stop, stand still, become stagnate, regress, find ourselves where we were on page one of our story, or we can continue moving toward what we truly want. Change. Grow. Enjoy the journey of the rewards of our labor. Reach our ultimate vision, goals, and dreams for our life.

Now, we must choose our direction, I hope you will continue with me, advancing in pursuit of your royal rendezvous.

Well-Suited

Progressing ahead, we seek to discover and follow the next directive from Isaiah. He tells the previously incarcerated one, "…*Clothe yourself with strength. Put on your garments of splendor*" (Isa. 52:1).

The third step in our process toward completion and wholeness is to COLLECT. You might be asking, "Collect what?" Let's explore.

Isaiah tells this now free woman to *put on* the right clothing. As we cast our gaze toward our former captive, we see she is standing outside the prison. However, her neck is marked, rash-red and bruised from the fetters of her previous condition. Her face is flushed, and her body is sweaty and grimy from her struggle for freedom. Her clothes are old, worn, and tattered. Although she is standing outside the walls of her former captivity, she is only halfway to freedom. She needs salve for her wounds and to be bathed. She needs a new wardrobe.

Removing the old is not enough. If all we do is remove what once was, we have only done half the work. When the past has been removed and is gone, replacing it with fresh, new, well-fitted garments is necessary for moving forward with the process. We must choose the replacement garments purposefully. If we are not intentional about the replacements, we will unintentionally allow, new, poorly fashioned mindsets to replace old, ill-fitting mindsets. We must set the vision before us and calculate what is required to accomplish that ultimate desire.

To eradicate old mindsets, we must replace them with beliefs that are true and correct about ourselves. We must collect the *right* information about ourselves. We need to *put on* the right heart, the right attitudes, and right thinking about ourselves. We need to correct our understanding about our identity; who we are in Christ, our value to God, and the world around us.

Isaiah instructs this daughter, and us, to dress appropriately. How do we know we have put on the right attire? There are other Scriptures which will aid us in our quest for collecting the appropriate garments.

The Scripture from Paul's letter to the Ephesians helps us with this understanding. Paul wrote to this group of believers,

> In reference to your former manner of life, you lay aside the old self, which is being corrupted in accordance with the lusts of deceit and that you be renewed in the spirit of your mind and put on the new self, which in the likeness of God has been created in righteousness and holiness of the truth. (Eph. 4:22-24 NASB)

There are two issues at stake in Paul's letter, as well as in Isaiah's account. They are the same issues at stake for us—the past and the future.

Both men stated there are two stages—before and after. As we read further into their writing, we see they also supplied both pieces of the remedy. Isaiah said to stand, shake off the dust, and remove the chains. Paul said to lay aside the old, corrupted self. In other words, both men instructed their followers to remove the old garments.

In the natural progression of things, both men instructed that the old must be replaced with something different. Paul said to put on the *new self*. Isaiah said to put on the correct garments, *garments of splendor*. So, how do I know whether I am wearing the right things to fit my new self?

When we clean out our closets, usually it is because we need to get rid of items that no longer fit or no longer suit the needs of our life. I do a closet cleanout at least once each year. It is healthy for me to shed those irrelevant items, and it can be helpful to others when I make the items available for someone else's use.

Following that practice, several years ago, I was going through my closet because I had accumulated excess. It was time to relinquish those items into someone else's care. Pulling out each piece, I began to create stacks—keep, toss, give away, etc. As I dug through to the shelves in the back of my closet, I found a special item. It was one of the souvenirs I had kept from high school because of the sentimental value, as well as a life lesson it represented.

During my high school years, western wear was in fashion, and I enjoyed wearing it. A heavily starched, oxford cloth shirt tucked into an even more heavily starched and creased pair of boot-cut jeans with cowboy boots peeking out and pointing the way—that was a basic western ensemble. I would accessorize that with a bolo tie or a coordinating skinny bowtie slipped through the button-down collar. Long and curly, BIG hair (remember, I *am* a Texan) flowed around my shoulders, and around my waist was wrapped with a tooled leather belt—my name stamped and painted on the back—complete with a large brass buckle. I topped off the ensemble with a western blazer, and I was ready for the style of the time. This description probably gives away my age, too, but you get the picture. That closet cleanout day, I uncovered my extraordinary tooled leather belt.

This belt was, and still is, of great value to me, for several reasons. First, I bought it at one of the finest stores in Amarillo that specialized in western apparel. Secondly, when I bought it, my best friend's older brother worked at the store, and he stamped my name onto the back of the belt. I love color, and I wanted my name in red. So, I asked him to paint my name in deep crimson to match the floral insets on the front of the belt. He smiled at me, wide and toothy, and said he was happy to do so.

Finally, the belt represented a life lesson for me. When I was in high school, I worked at a fast food restaurant. I earned a few cents more than $3 per hour and worked nights and weekends. My parents were the type to find every opportunity for me and my siblings to learn about handling responsibility at an early age, including fiscal responsibility. While they provided a car for me, it was my obligation to purchase all the gasoline, give to the work of the church, deposit a portion of my income into a savings account, pay for my clothing and extras, and provide my own spending money. I desperately wanted that western belt, but it cost $29.95, plus tax, and the fee to have it stamped and painted. Working diligently, it took me several two-week pay periods to save enough extra cash to buy the coveted belt. I reached the financial goal and was immensely proud when I could walk in the store and buy my belt.

The thick leather laid worn and soft on my fingers, as I held my personalized belt on that closet cleanout day. I reminisced about the warm, sunny day my best friend, Carlenia, and I drove to the store so I could make that purchase and appreciated the reminder of its significance to me. To bring a little sparkle of fun to my closet cleaning, I decided to put on the belt and wear it while I continued cleaning out the remaining attire. So, I slipped it off the loop of the belt hanger, and wrapped it around my waist, over my outfit.

Uh. Wait. What is that? What just happened? Oh. Well, I *used* to wear the belt at the smallest loop, but here I was buckling it on the second one from the end. Hmmmm…two children, four major surgeries, and twenty-plus years later, my belt no longer fit the same. My heart sank a little, but for only a moment or two.

Here is what I know. Change happens. Change does not always require growth, but growth *always* requires change.

When we have a weight change, we usually experience a subsequent size adjustment. With an adjustment to our size, we develop a need to rid ourselves of clothing in our old size and bring in garments in the new. The same thing happens when we have a lifestyle change. When we change professions, often our wardrobe changes—either to a more tailored and fitted style, or a more relaxed one. When we retire, wardrobe requirements readjust altogether.

Our daughter of Zion had to make a profound and weighty (forgive the pun) adjustment to her wardrobe. It was time for her not only to rid herself of what she had been wearing for such an extended period, but she needed to replace those items with the appropriate garments. Isaiah instructed her that strength and beauty were the garments she needed.

> *Change does not always require growth, but growth always requires change.*

As with our clothing, replacing our mindsets is necessary when we come to the realization that they are not suited to our best life. To clothe ourselves with strength and beauty, we must collect the right information about ourselves. This collection includes the correct information about all our relationships. When we are in right relationship with God, then all our other relationships will begin to change and improve, as well—family, friendships, workplace, and community. Most importantly, our right relationship with God corrects, rectifies and reconciles our relationship with our self. Our heart and mind will understand we do *not* define our identity by circumstances that have occurred in our life. Our identity is *not* limited by occurrences to which other people have subjected us. The opinions of others do *not* define our identity. Our identity is *not* determined by where we have been or what we have experienced. Instead, our identity is characterized by who we are, and more importantly, *whose* we are.

As we delve into this idea of collecting and putting on the right garments, I want to describe the heart and mind in biblical terms. The Hebrew word which is transliterated into English as *heart* or *mind* is the word *leb*. *Leb* refers to the inner person, the will, and the seat of appetites, emotions, and passions. It is it the *essence* of an individual. In other words, the *leb* is the essence of who we are.

When we talk about changing our heart and mind from incorrect thinking to correct thinking, we are talking about the transformation of understanding who we are.

As I have shared, my greatest hindrance to living a fulfilled, purposeful life was fear. When awakened in the night from the childhood nightmares, I found myself breathing heavily and gasping for air, from running and crying while asleep. In the scenario of these terrorizing dreams, like our daughter in Isaiah's account, my hands and feet were free, so that I could run. However, the breath of life was being sucked out of me because a dark robe of fear was chained to my neck. Fear was the thing I wanted to be removed from my life forever. It was a dusty, worn, smelly, and tattered garment I needed to detach and eliminate.

We have established the truth that we cannot grow without changing. Growth *always* requires change, which means we cannot avoid changing and evolving if we want to improve ourselves on any level. When we want to be healthier, we must change our mindset regarding our diet, sleep, and exercise habits. When we want to increase our productivity, we must change our philosophy about busyness and time management. Improving our level of spiritual and personal success works the same way. Change is required. We must augment our core beliefs regarding ourselves and our identity in God through Christ Jesus. When we intensify our relationship with Jesus, we will have the necessary information to do things differently, thereby gaining the results we want.

The Beveled Edge

Everyone who takes a first glance does not see the beauty contained within a rough slab of stone. A trained eye must explore the walls of a cave and the sides of a rock formation before a cave can become a mine. When the miner finds the deposit that holds the vein of cherished stone, this extensive excavation process begins. The miner carefully and cautiously starts chipping around the vein containing the prized deposit with a pickaxe, cutting slabs of stone to cart out of the mine. The artisan takes the piece and removes the rough, then begins sawing, grinding, sanding, and watering. Then, sawing and grinding gain, sanding once more, the artisan crafts. Eventually, as the water washes away the sand, the innate beauty arises from the dark stone as light filters through from one side to another. The gem is ready for its next procedure.

Facets are the angles made at the edges of the stone. When a lapidary cuts a gem for setting, the stone is faceted on every surface. He shapes and crafts the gem specially to the stone itself. The artisan sees the stone's potential and begins cutting it into the shape it was created to reveal. As we admire it from the top, the gemstone glistens. However, the stone is not only cut on the top but also faceted at various angles on the sides and the bottom. Each surface is sliced at the exact angle to best capture the light and then bend it through the stone. When the top of the gemstone is cut, light bends as it passes through the facets. Each ray bounces off and compliments the others, awakening the sparkle, and revealing the brilliance and quality of the gem.

Similarly, our lives are faceted by cutting away our rough—those issues that drag us into the trash of life. The rough dulls our sheen and adds weight without value. So, the Lord, our

Lapidary, must continue working on us, steadily and consistently peeling away calloused fragments to reveal the soft flesh that reflects His image. With gentle kindness and compassionate patience, He places us on the post and begins to turn the wheel. As we are laid out before Him, like a skilled gem cutter, our Artisan begins slicing through with His abounding grace, beveling off the final edges of our ill-fitted rough. We can then stand, take hold of the blighted, flawed, dark segments of our past experiences, and remove them. From the moment those familiar dysfunctions fall away from us, like our daughter of Zion's old, tattered garments, the light of Christ Jesus shines through us more brilliantly. Our lives reveal the sparkle of Christ's joy.

This wardrobe change sets the horizon of our life aglow with the buttery gold glimmer of a positive renovation of the mind. Garments of strength and splendor replace the ragged fray of our past and transforming truth illuminates our world.

Spelunking the Mind Shift—Positive Attitude Toward Change and Changing

Our first mindset shift is the positive change that brings about transformation. At first glance, removing a piece of our experience, tattered though it is, may not appear to be positive. We may feel a sense of trepidation. However, we cannot allow the shady tinge of the fear of change to prevent us from moving forward, toward our ultimate goals, dreams, and vision. We need to stand firm in our resolve to improve, develop, and advance.

Each day, the decision lies before us whether we will choose to remain where we are or become better and more Christ-like. That means that today I have the potential to be more like Jesus than I was yesterday. Each morning, through the presence of the Holy Spirit, who is active in our life, we can begin the day communing with the Lord. As we worship and praise Him, we can declare to Him that this day we entrust our life into His care. As we pray and place our trust in the Lord, we also speak into our own experience the declaration that we choose to be better today than we were yesterday. The apostle Paul says it like this,

> Now the Lord is the Spirit, and where the Spirit of the Lord is, there is freedom. We all, with unveiled faces, are looking as in a mirror at the glory of the Lord and are being transformed into the same image from glory to glory; this is from the Lord who is the Spirit. (2 Cor. 3:17-18 HCSB)

The idea that we are being transformed into the image of Jesus, from glory to glory, means this is a continuous, ongoing process. In other words, we have the potential to do better, to achieve higher, to be *more*, through Christ, today, than we have been in the past, even as recently as yesterday, and we can look forward to being improved tomorrow from where we are today.

In our culture, we tend to attach a monetary value to success. However, spiritual and personal success is not about achieving an individual status, making a specific amount of money, driving a favorite car, living in a particular kind of dwelling, or any other type of material gain. Personal and spiritual success is about first entrusting ourselves to, and growing spiritually in, the Lord God, Creator of us. It is about surrendering ourselves to His will and purpose and pursuing that purpose for which He created us. When we do this, we will approach the changes necessary for transformation with the right heart attitude.

When we desire positive growth, desire is only the first part and is not enough in itself. Desire reveals clues that when followed, lead us toward the changes required of us to achieve the outcome we want. We have already acknowledged we possess the authority to take control of our thoughts, by capturing them and bringing them into the obedience of Christ, as Paul taught in 2 Corinthians 10:5. We need to take on the mindset that we not only desire change but are willing to take action to bring about that change.

Paul also wrote a letter to the Galatians to aid them in understanding the changes brought about through the indwelling presence of the Holy Spirit. Paul addresses what their lives were once like and lists several things that were prevalent in their former way of life. Then, he fills the Galatians with hope by revealing the manifestation of their new lifestyle. A life yielded entirely to the Lord is full of His presence, and overflows with a new crop of fruit. Paul wrote, "But the fruit of the Spirit is love, joy, peace, patience, kindness, goodness, faithfulness, gentleness, self-control; against such things there is no law" (Gal. 5:22-23 NASB).

What a beautiful, bumper crop of fabulous results we can have. The way we garner these tasty delights for our life is first to acknowledge our need for change. Then we must yield our self with the right heart attitude to the One who will fill us with His presence and guide us to the Truth. Then, we begin making changes. The results we see will be growth in our own life and spirit, sprouting the production of new, sweet fruit of the Holy Spirit.

With this background information about removing the old, former way of life and putting on the new way of life, it might help us to have the formula to achieve it. Our recipe is this: change, plus the right heart attitude, equals positive growth. When we keep our focus on the goal and grow toward it, we will achieve the vision for our life.

Order from Chaos

As the apostle Paul described the former way of life for the Galatians, one cannot help but perceive how chaotic their lives must have been before their understanding about Jesus—His life and sacrifice, His resurrection, and the indwelling presence of His Holy Spirit. Once they accepted the Truth of Jesus, His identity as the Savior of the world, and their ability to know Him, everything in their lives transformed into something new. Lives, once characterized by muddled pandemonium, had become a beautiful work of artistry.

Our daughter of Zion had known a lifetime of entangled imprisonment in a mess of her own making. She had wandered far from what she knew was the best way. With each decision to rebel and move further away from her Creator, our daughter proceeded in the wrong direction, and her fetters tightened. She found herself a captive of her abysmal choices, making her weak, wretched, enslaved, dirty, chained, and gasping for air. Isaiah revealed to her that her life could change. She could remove the chains of chaos from her life. Learning from her situation, we find the same is true for us, whether we are in a mess of our own making or subjected to the results of the tumultuous doings of another.

The steps in the procession to our royal rendezvous will both overlap, and work in conjunction while being applied to each situation. Still they must be applied in order: CONFRONT, COLLAPSE, COLLECT, CONVERT, and CONNECT. We cannot take the last three steps until we confront and collapse the wrong things. Eliminating incorrect, inaccurate, and limiting beliefs, then collecting correct beliefs about our self, about who we are, and the truth of our purpose is our growth goal. Adjusting our thoughts about our self helps us make this crucial exchange.

When we make this exchange, we will find we can have peace in place of pandemonium. We can discover direction out of disarray. We can replace turmoil and commotion with stability and confidence. And, we have the authority to create order out of chaos.

Garments of Splendor

Faith

The first component of our new collection is *faith*. When we distill the definition of faith, we can define it as complete trust and belief in something, especially with firm conviction, even when there is no proof.[6] The Bible describes faith this way: "Now faith is the assurance (title deed, confirmation) of things hoped for (divinely guaranteed), and the evidence of things not seen [the conviction of their reality—faith comprehends as fact what cannot be experienced by the physical senses]" (Heb. 11:1 AMP).

When we break down this Scripture, grammatically, we can see the definition of *faith* more readily, as given by the writer. The first phrase says, "Now *faith* is the *assurance.*" *Assurance* is joined to the words "the *evidence*" by the conjunction "and." By this, we know the writer of the book of Hebrews says *faith is the assurance* and *the evidence*. This *assurance* is the knowledge of or knowing something, and *evidence* is the associated result or action. Using this definition, let's look at what it means to *collect faith*, to grow in our spiritual and personal success.

To *collect faith* means to believe correctly about our self in relation to God, family, workplace, and community. We discard incorrect beliefs about our worth and value, exchanging them for correct beliefs about ourselves—faith that we are *assured* of who we are in relation to God, we are *assured* of our identity in Christ, and we are *assured* we have a place reserved in God's Kingdom with a God-given purpose to fulfill.[7]

With this assurance then, we begin collecting and fully grasping the reality that we are valuable to God, and that He offers us incalculable worth in Christ. The *evidence* of our faith manifests when we realize God offers us power, authority, and control over mistaken beliefs about ourselves, and we take authority over them. The presence of the Holy Spirit helps us thoroughly remove these inaccuracies from our thought processes. Although people cannot see the Holy Spirit actually at work in us, they can see the *evidence* of His work in our changed attitudes and actions. My faith (assurance) is placed in the Lord; the result (evidence) is my transforming life.

Placing my faith in God through Jesus Christ, I have direct access to God. He never removes my free will to make choices. I retain the power of choice. He gives me the opportunity and authority to exercise my free will and choose to control my thoughts, by "...taking every thought captive to the obedience of Christ" (2 Cor. 10:5 NASB). Do you see the pattern? I have referred to this particular Scripture three times. I am emphasizing this precise Scripture because I want us to grasp fully the veracity of the reality that we have been given complete authority of our thought life.

There is one word of paramount importance in the first verse from Hebrews 11:1 that we have not yet explored. That word is *now*. Our faith can become active right *now*; it is the time to make the changes necessary to live a purposeful, intentional life. We can put our faith to work right *now*.

Power

An addition to our updated apparel is *power*. We replace our false beliefs with the knowledge of our strength in Christ. For me—and for all those who like me have had a personal relationship with fear—this means I have *power* over fear. The phrase *fear not*, or some derivative of it appears in Scripture 366 times. That is good news for someone who is, or has been, bound by fear. Isaiah declared, "Behold, God is my Salvation; I will trust, and will not be afraid; for the LORD GOD is my strength and my song, and He has become my salvation" (Isa. 12:2 ESV).

Faith and power work hand in hand. Exercising our faith in God through our relationship with Christ increases our understanding of the power we possess in Him.

Bejeweled Scepter of Choice, Authority, and Control

We must also include among our new garments the three-channeled scepter, bejeweled with choice, authority, and control. It is pivotal when we replace our incorrect beliefs with the knowledge that we have the power and *control* of our minds. As we have discussed, the apostle Paul instructed the people of Galatia that the Holy Spirit dwelling within them would be shown in their actions as a fruitful yield, borne out by their heart attitudes. One fruit Paul listed is *self-control*. We do not have to be overcome by circumstance. We possess the ability to control our response in every situation.

The power of *choice* accompanies authority and control. I have the power of influence and control, in Christ, over my thoughts. I have the ability, authority, and control to *choose* the subjects to which I give thought time, those things upon which I meditate.

When we adorn our garments with the power of choice by exercising authority and control over our thoughts, then we put on these beautiful garments of *right thinking*. We do this by intentionally choosing what we put into our minds from this moment forward. For example, we can make positive choices regarding media programming for listening and watching, as well as printed and electronic media we select for reading. In Paul's letter to the Philippians, he directly addressed those things that are good for our minds. Paul wrote, "…whatever is true, whatever is noble, whatever is right, whatever is pure, whatever is lovely, whatever is admirable—if anything is excellent or praiseworthy—think about such things" (Phil. 4:8).

Paul wrote to the Philippians to fix their minds and aim their focus on these positive things. In the New American Standard Bible, the phrase is translated to "dwell on these things." To *dwell* means to live in a particular place, to take up residence in that place. In other words, this Scripture is teaching us to live with the mindset of thinking on what is right, all the time. We can transform the fruit of our lives by sending our thoughts to move in to and take up residence in the house of excellent thinking. Negative, self-limiting, self-prohibiting, and subsequently destructive thoughts have no room to live when we fill our minds with good, positive, excellent, and praiseworthy thinking.

Robe of Strength

Our ancient Old Testament trainer, Isaiah, coaches us to put on *strength*. A strength trainer will tell his trainee they cannot put on, all at once, the strength they need for supporting a more significant load. Instead, a person must build up his or her power to carry the full amount required. When we increase or put on strength, it is an exercise in building muscle, stamina, and endurance. Likewise, when we put on the strength to which Isaiah refers, we begin by putting on correct thoughts about ourselves, and our identity in the Lord.

When we refer back to our Scripture from Isaiah, the command is to put on *strength* and *beautiful garments*. The more we exercise our choice to wear the garments of *faith* and *power* and reorder our thoughts to focus on the subjects of *right thinking*—things that are excellent, pleasant, peaceful, and inspire growth—the less room there is available for fear, or other self-limiting beliefs.

As we continue to collect faith by exercising it, we will discover the power we have available to us in Christ. By stretching and strengthening that faith in Christ, we stimulate our knowledge and understanding of His power at work in us. Through this acquired knowledge, we bolster our strength in Jesus, enabling us to comprehend that through Christ we can indeed carry the weight of the work we need to do and accomplish it because His power is at work in us. "For it is God who is working in you, enabling you both to desire and to work out His good purpose" (Phil. 2:13 HCSB).

As the Lord was moving me through this process out of many years of fear, I applied these Scriptures to my life more fervently than ever before. The natural result was an increasing level of faith. Subsequently, as faith increased, the frequency of applying the new way of thinking to my life also improved. The ultimate result of this ever-increasing faith and transformational mindset was the ability to progress where I had a desire to succeed but had previously been too fearful to try. I was experiencing the ongoing process of being transformed.

Glimmers of the Crown

I have been crucified with Christ. It is no longer I who live, but Christ who lives in me. And the life I now live in the flesh I live by faith in the Son of God, who loved me and gave himself for me. (Gal. 2:20 ESV)

But if You can do anything, have compassion on us and help us. And Jesus said to him, "'If you can'! All things are possible for one who believes." Immediately the father of the child cried out and said, "I believe; help my unbelief!" (Mark 9:22b-24 ESV)

God is our refuge and strength, an ever-present help in trouble. Therefore, we will not fear…He says, "Be still, and know that I am God; I will be exalted among the nations, I will be exalted in the earth." (Psa. 46:1, 2a, 10 NIV)

For nothing will be impossible with God. (Luke 1:37 ESV)

Trust in and rely confidently on the Lord with all your heart, and do not rely on your own insight or understanding. In all your ways know and acknowledge and recognize Him, And He will make your paths straight and smooth [removing obstacles that block your way]. (Prov. 3:5-6 AMP)

CHAPTER 6

Fresh Lips — Everyone Needs A Little Gloss

Because of our daughter of Zion's extended period of imprisonment and knowing that she was clad in soiled layers of dust and grime, we can postulate the probability that she was under-hydrated during her incarceration. She was probably thirsty to the point of exhaustion, leaving her skin rough and scaly, peeling at her elbows, and flaking around her muck encrusted ankles. Perhaps her gaunt face, with a furrowed brow and hollowed eyes, divulged the wearing of fear and worry. Her heart's only song was the lament of mourning over her plight. Her teeth—weakened from lack of nutrients—longed to bite and chew. Her tongue yearned to taste the delicious flavors of lamb again, with herbs, olives, and figs. Her timeworn mouth was drawn and creased from thirst, and the edges were whitened with the foam of salty sweat and dried saliva. Her parched lips were like an old rawhide. They were chapped, cracked, and bleeding.

Our daughter of Zion needed a drink. She needed a long, soothing swallow from the only fountain that could slake her dehydrated body and scorched soul. She desperately needed the Fountain of Life to refresh, renew, and restore.

What brought her to this arid prison? How could her thirst be so forsaken?

Like our daughter of Zion, we are weary and worn. Our heart's song dulls with the scorn of our toxic rumination, its chords entirely out of tune with our deepest longing. This prison of our mind has locked us in the dreary cellblock of our negative thoughts. It has left us trapped in the muck of dry, dirty, destructive beliefs. We yearn for the comforting gulp of healing and are ready to trade our prison, for that refreshment we so desperately need.

How did we arrive at this withered gulch in life? How could we be so bone dry?

There is something we carry with us, always, that can make or break us. When we find ourselves in a place of desert dryness with no oasis in sight, we can point back to this small piece of our adornment, knowing it played a role in getting us here. When properly outfitted, this tiny accoutrement will take us to magnificent places beyond our imagination. When dripping with fly-ridden rot, it can drop us into a bottomless pit with no escape. What is this estuary that carries such a flow of power? It holds what the Biblical writer, James, called "a restless evil, full of deadly poison." (James 3:8) This powerful muscle is the tongue. James reveals how a person can bring a blessing or cursing upon his or her own life by their speech and addresses the reality that we all stumble in what we say.

If anyone does not stumble in what he says, he is a mature man who is also able to control his whole body…though the tongue is a small part of the body, it boasts great things. Consider how large a forest a small fire ignites. And the tongue is a fire…It pollutes the whole body, sets the course of life on fire…no man can tame the tongue. It is a restless evil, full of deadly poison. We praise our Lord and Father with it, and we curse men who are made in God's likeness with it. Praising and cursing come out of the same mouth. (James 3:2b-10a HCSB)

It is conceivable our daughter of Zion opened her mouth and wielded her tongue with vile negativity and scorn in such a way as to bring a curse upon herself. Perhaps we are guilty of doing the same thing—speaking negatively toward ourselves in such a way that we keep the bars of our prison locked securely in place.

It is time for us to add a new mouth to our collection. We must form and fashion new lips. We find this renewed mouth and refreshing of our lips by placing them at the flow of the fountain of life. It is at this fountain we may open lips, unhinged, to sing a new song. Let us look to the psalmist, as he tells us where we can find this clear, cold, life-giving drink. "They drink their fill of the abundance of Your house; And You give them to drink of the river of Your delights. For with You is the fountain of life; In Your light we see light" (Ps. 36:8-9 NASB). This Scripture reveals that we find the Lord's fountain where He dwells, "*of Your house*" and "*in Your light*." The Lord dwells in His house, but where exactly is that?

In the book of Genesis, when time was first recorded as the space between evening and morning, we are shown that God dwelled and communed with His Creation. In the Garden of Eden, the Lord physically walked and talked with Adam and Eve, and the account states that God looked for them in the cool, evening breezes of the day (Gen. 3:8).

When they disobeyed Him and ate the fruit from the Tree of the Knowledge of Good and Evil, their sin (disobedience to God's ordinance) separated them from God's presence. It was then that all of creation became cursed. At that point, God chose to dwell with man on a limited basis. He made regular contact with His people in the confines of the Holy of Holies, within the interior of the Tent of Meeting, or during tabernacle. Later, King Solomon constructed the Temple, at God's direction, where, again, the Lord would dwell in the Holy of Holies. Still, that was not enough.

From the beginning, God had a perfect plan for humanity's redemption. He sent His son, Jesus, who is the Messiah, the anointed One, the Christ. Jesus came to live, teach, and become the supreme sacrifice, for the restoration of people back to God. Upon His crucifixion, and through His resurrection, Jesus defeated death, hell, and the grave, and He provided redemption for all of humanity. The shed blood of Jesus Christ bought humankind's ability to be reconciled into right relationship with God and call upon Him directly. When Jesus left the earth after His resurrection, He promised to send the comforter, who is the Holy Spirit. Through the indwelling of His Holy Spirit, God now resides—dwells—within the heart of each person who has entrusted their life to Him completely and without reservation.

The only way we can quench the thirsting of our souls is to pursue the Lord, in every part of our lives, including the way we speak.

Do we ever listen to ourselves? Do we listen to the things we say? What about listening to *how* we speak? Where are the inflections in the voice? Do we weigh our words before we release them? Or, do we give voice to our thoughts, discharging them into the atmosphere, expecting the hearer to receive them as intended, and presuming anything unnecessary will vaporize?

There is a sobering truth each of us must understand. We are accountable for *everything* we say, and that includes what we say to ourselves. In Matthew's account of the Gospel, Jesus told His disciples, "But I tell you that everyone will have to give account on the day of judgment for every empty word they have spoken. For by your words you will be acquitted, and by your words you will be condemned" (Matt. 12:36-37) The word *empty* in this Scripture is also translated as *idle*, *careless*, or *useless*.

Throughout the Bible, the writers gave strong admonition about our speech. In Paul's letter to the Ephesians, he gave a lengthy discourse about the behavior of one who claims to be in Christ. In it, Paul included several statements about a person's speech. He said, "Do not let any unwholesome talk come out of your mouths, but only what is helpful for building others up according to their needs, that it may benefit those who listen" (Eph. 4:29).

The emphasis of this warning is in three phases. Paul begins by giving a directive of what not to say—*anything unwholesome*. *The Amplified Bible* elaborates unwholesome in the following way: "… foul or polluting … evil … unwholesome or worthless…" When we look at this closely, we understand the negative words we speak to ourselves are foul to our spirit. Negative self-talk brings our dishonor. Our adverse words can be damaging to us because they are not healthy, nutritious, or nourishing to our soul.

Paul, however, does not leave us in that undesirable place of loathsome speech. He leads us from the objectionable speech to where we can and should be, in the way we speak. Paul says the words we utter should be helpful and encouraging, as well as beneficial and gracious. He said, "… but only what is helpful for building others up … that it may benefit those who listen." In *The Amplified Bible* this is rendered, "… but only such [speech] as is good and beneficial to the spiritual progress of others ... that it may be a blessing and give grace (God's favor) to those who hear it."

When we speak negatively about our self, we inhibit our spiritual progress. Our negative words neither bless, help, encourage, nor give grace. Rather, they curse. Thus, we curse ourselves with our negative words.

The foremost Scripture about the impact of our words is the wisdom delivered by King Solomon when he said, "From the fruit of his mouth a man's stomach is satisfied; he is filled with the product of his lips. Life and death are in the power of the tongue, and those who love it will eat its fruit" (Prov. 18:20-21 HCSB).

The words we speak are weighty. They carry considerable power. Our words can bring either life or death to our conversation, as well as to our spirit. We need to be aware that our words do not evaporate. Words are not benign. Instead, they muscle influence and sway. In each instance of speech (spoken, written, or typed), our words will come back to us for our consumption.

Are our lips desert dry, bearing words of empty, vain self-loathing? You may be asking why I said, "*vain* self-loathing," so let me explain. The majority of people think about themselves in terms of their failures. We tend to focus our attention on what we do wrong. We may say things such as: "I never say the right thing," "I am so stupid," "I don't like the way I look because of _____ (fill in the blank)," "I wish I could do this thing _____ right (fill in the blank)," "Why am I at this job? I don't even know what I'm doing," "My spouse thinks I'm inept at _____ (fill in the blank)," or "Everyone thinks I'm not good at _____ (fill in the blank)." When we are continually thinking about how lowly we are, how underserving, we are still only thinking of our self. So, it becomes a self-centered vanity on the negative side.

When we speak those things into the atmosphere, a cycle begins. Those things come directly back into our hearing, whether we are talking to another person, mumbling frustrations to the person in the mirror, or muttering under our breath while we complete a task. The cycle begins with a negative thought and continues when we expel and give voice to those thoughts in the form of words. Our words touch the atmosphere. We hear our own words bouncing back to us. Those words go directly back into our soul, and then it all starts over again, growing in intensity with each cycle.

Additionally, if we speak negative words to another person, we affect their thoughts, their mind, their soul, and their opinion. As we speak these negative words, we create and enter into a cycle of negative thinking. With each negative statement spoken against our self, we intensify and grow the negativity toward ourselves, and continue to devalue our worth.

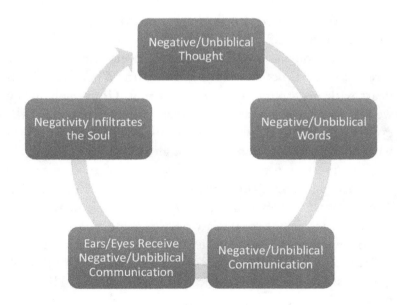

In Luke's account of the Gospel, he records an occasion of Jesus speaking to a large crowd gathered on a plain. He was addressing people from various backgrounds, including

Pharisees, as well as different Gentile groups. Jesus said, "The good person out of the good treasure of his heart produces good, and the evil person out of his evil treasure produces evil, for out of the abundance of the heart his mouth speaks" (Luke 6:45 ESV). Jesus was speaking about the hypocritical difference between the way people would talk and the way they lived. This was particularly true of the Pharisees. We must ask whether we are guilty of the same thing when we fill our mind with the cycle of negative thoughts and harmful speech about our value, then try to pass off publicly that we are "fine," "great," or "doing well." On the outside, we appear okay, reasonable, and put together. Inside, we are self-loathing, frustrated, hurt, angry, and miserable.

The reality for us is this: we become the way we think about ourselves. King Solomon recorded in his many proverbs, "Above all else, guard your heart, for everything you do flows from it" (Prov. 4:23).

Think about Solomon's statement. Everything we do is a direct result of the contents of our heart. When we fill our heart with negativity, we will act on that. Conversely, when we fill our heart with what is correct, we will act on that. The cycle works the same way when we fill our hearts and minds with positive Christ-centered thoughts.

The question for us then is, *What kind of lips do we wear?*

Throughout the Psalms, there is a unifying theme of praise. The psalmist adores, exalts, extols, glorifies, and worships God. In each instance of his worship, the psalmist is doing one of two things. The psalmist in some passages is speaking to Jehovah God, telling Him of his understanding of God's greatness, His power, His justice, His righteousness, His faithfulness, His gentleness, His compassion, and His many other attributes. In other passages, the psalmist is speaking to the people, encouraging and compelling them to join together to sing, praise, shout, exalt, worship, and make the name of the Lord great among the people.

Psalms also reveals at times, in rather raw terms, the conditions of the life of the psalmist. David wrote psalms when he was in the worst of circumstances, whether created through his poor judgment and sinful behavior or when amid warfare and surrounded by his enemies. Even in such dire situations, David chose to bring glory to God. He acknowledged God's sovereignty, confessed his sins to Him, and asked to be cleansed. David thanked, praised, and worshiped God for His goodness, love, forgiveness, and protection.

Over and again, we read in the Psalms the declaration "I will." The choice was clear to willingly honor, glorify, praise, and worship Jehovah God, no matter what else was happening in the life of the psalmist.

Putting praise on our lips occurs only by making a conscious decision to do so. Again, this reveals a mindset. Choosing to look for that which is praiseworthy, and then centering our communication on it begins with how we think.

Declarations About Our Mindset

I want to take some time to address a specific point about all this modification in our thinking, particularly about our self-talk.

There is a widespread practice called *positive affirmation*. This practice is when a person systematically and repeatedly writes down and speaks aloud the things they want for their life. You may be a practitioner of this. If so, what I am about to say may surprise you, so keep reading if it does. We cannot merely apply positive affirmations to our days and expect that to be the end-all.

The reason for my statement is that positive affirmations as commonly known and taught are not a biblical concept. While the affirmations are considered *spiritual*, the practice is derived through the mystical type teachings of the New Age or New Thought movements (both of which are decidedly not Christian). From Wikipedia, the online free encyclopedia, affirmations are defined as follows:

> Affirmations in New Thought and New Age terminology refer primarily to the practice of positive thinking and self-empowerment – fostering a belief that "a positive mental attitude supported by affirmations will achieve success in anything." More specifically, an affirmation is a carefully formatted statement that should be repeated to one's self and written down frequently. For affirmations to be effective, it is said that they need to be present tense, positive, personal and specific.[8,9]

Positive affirmations are only about the self, one's ego, and one's ability, in and of the self, to become a better person.

From a Christ-centered, biblical perspective, we—believers in and followers of Jesus Christ—understand we are innately not good because we are born with the nature of sin (Ps. 51:5; Rom. 3:9-18, 23; 1 John 1:8), and therefore, we alone cannot make ourselves better, especially by the mere practice of making positive statements about ourselves.

In his letter to the Philippians, when Paul listed examples of those things upon which we should fix our minds and meditate, he was not discussing generalized, positive affirmations centered on what makes a person feel happy. Instead, Paul was speaking to the fact that as Christ followers, we need to set our thoughts and minds on the things that are pleasing to Christ.

In the world's system and culture, achieving and accumulating things such as a better job, a bigger house, higher education, a newer car, more wealth, coveted titles, prominent status, and enviable positions all hold high importance. We should seek to be happy and take care of number one—ourselves—first. For the Christ follower, the importance of one's self and the desire for self-indulgence diminishes as one's relationship with Jesus grows. Paul stated we need to direct our focus on the things that are nobler and higher than those things of this life. When we place our faith in the Lord and entrust our self to His care and calling, then we will focus on what He wants for us. Those things are true, noble, right, pure, lovely, admirable, excellent, and praiseworthy, in the *Lord's sight*, but not necessarily in the sight of our peers. As we focus on His desire for a flourishing thought life, our mind will experience transformation with improved ability to address the issues of life which present themselves from time to time.

The affirmations we want to load into our minds are those things God says about Himself and those things the Word reveals to us about our identity in God through Jesus Christ.

What the Bible Reveals About God

The following list of truths about God's identity is revealed to us throughout the Bible. Though this is not an exhaustive list, knowing these wonderful attributes about God helps us better understand His magnificence. Because He reveals these things about Himself to us, we know we can trust Him with all we are, and we can confidently expect Him to fulfill all we need.

1. God is infinite, self-existent, and has no beginning or end (Col. 1:17; John 5:26).

2. God never changes (Mal. 3:16)

3. God is all powerful and nothing is beyond His ability (Ps. 33:6; 24:8; Job 11:7-11; Heb. 6:18; Gen. 18:14; Jer. 32:17, 27; Luke 1:37; 2 Cor. 6:18; Rev. 1:8; Eph. 3:20).

4. God is life (Job 12:7-10).

5. God knows all things (Ps. 33:11-13; Isa. 46:9-10).

6. God is everywhere, all the time (Ps. 137; 139:7-10; Jer. 23:23-24).

7. God is spirit (Num. 23:19; John 4:24).

8. God is wise and perfect (2 Sam. 22:27-37; Ps. 18:30; Rom. 11:33).

9. God is true and faithful (Num. 23:19; Deut. 7:9; 2 Tim. 2:13).

10. God is good (Ps. 34:8; 84:11-12; James 1:17).

11. God is righteous, just, and perfect in all His doings (Deut. 32:4; Ps. 50:6; 116:5).

12. God saves (Ps. 68:19-20; John 3:16-17; Rom. 6:23).

13. God is merciful, compassionate, and kind (Ex. 34:5-7; Deut. 4:24-31; Lam. 3:22-23; Mic. 7:18-19; Rom. 9:15-16).

14. God is gracious (Ex. 33:19; 2 Chron. 30:8-9; Ps. 145:8; Matt. 5:45; Eph. 2:8).

15. God is patient with us (2 Pet. 3:9).

16. God is light (1 John 1:5).

17. God is loving (John 3:16-17; 1 John 4:7-9).

18. God is with us and does not leave us (Deut. 31:6; Josh. 1:8-9; Heb. 13:5).

19. God is Sovereign (Deut. 10:12-22; Isa. 40:23).

20. God is victorious (Deut. 20:1-4; John 16:33; Rom. 8:31-32; Prov. 21:31; 1 Cor. 15:55-57).

21. God is holy and perfect (Rev. 4:8; Matt. 5:48).

22. God is beautiful (Hab. 3:4).

23. There is no god like the I AM (Deut. 6:4-5; 2 Sam. 22:32-34).

What the Bible Reveals About Who We Are to God in Christ

The truths about who we are to God, in Christ, are also shown throughout the Bible. The following is not an exhaustive list, but these are some of the truths we can know about ourselves when we entrust our lives to God, in Christ.

1. We are made in His image and have a purpose to fulfill (Gen. 1:27; Jer. 1:5; Ps. 139; Eph. 2:10).

2. We are justified and redeemed in Christ (Rom. 3:24; Eph. 1:7; 2:13).

3. We are accepted by Christ (Rom. 15:7).

4. We are alive in Christ (Eph. 2:4-5).

5. We are made God's children through Christ (John 1:12; Rom. 8:17; Gal. 4:7; Eph. 1:5; 1 John 3:1-2).

6. We are united with Him and one with Him in spirit (Gal. 3:27-28; 1 Cor. 6:17).

7. We are part of the body of Christ and have His life in ourselves (John 15:1,5; 1 Cor. 12:27; Eph. 3:6).

8. We are free in Christ (Gal. 5:1).

9. We are His friend (John 15:15).

10. We are His temple (1 Cor. 6:19-20).

11. We have power over sin (Rom. 6:6; 8:2).

12. We are His people and citizens of His Kingdom (Phil. 3:20; 1 Pet. 2:9).

13. We are called to be His holy saints (Lev. 11:44-45; 1 Cor. 1:2; Eph. 1:4; 1 Pet. 1:16).

14. He will care for us and meet all our needs (Matt. 6:25-33; Phil. 4:19; Eph. 3:20).

15. He gives us wisdom (1 Cor. 1:30; James 1:5-7).

16. We are victorious in Christ (Rom. 8:37; 2 Cor. 2:14; 1 John 5:1-4).

17. We are new in Christ (2 Cor. 5:17).

18. Our minds are renewed in Christ (2 Cor. 3:14; Rom. 12:1-2).

19. We are the righteousness of God in Christ (2 Cor. 5:21).

20. We are blessed in Christ (Eph. 1:3).

21. We are sealed in Christ (Eph. 1:13).

22. We are complete in Christ (Col. 2:10).

Glimmers of the Crown

Through the writings of John, the Word of God teaches us the result of being Christ's followers—devoted to the truth and walking with Him—is the ability to access His power and provision. That means, we will be physically, mentally, and spiritually prosperous, as our soul is prospering in Him.

> Beloved, I pray that in every way you may succeed and prosper and be in good health [physically], just as [I know] your soul prospers [spiritually]. For I was greatly pleased when [some of the] brothers came [from time to time] and testified to your [faithfulness to the] truth [of the gospel message], that is, how you are walking in truth. I have no greater joy than this, to hear that my [spiritual] children are living [their lives] in the truth. (3 John 1:2-4 AMP)

PART 4

Convert

The uncircumcised and defiled
will not enter you again

CHAPTER 7

Polish—Sand and Water

The lapidarist of our life is on the last step of His artistry. Like chunks of stone faceted away from a valuable gem, our artisan has sliced away, with meticulous precision, and removed from us the heart callouses of our old way of thinking. Extending gentle strokes as cushiony as luxuriously soft, new wool, He now wipes us clean. From His prized gem He pushes away the residue of tiny particles of sand. He washes His cherished jewel with living water, flushing away the minute shrapnel from the wheeling of the grindstone. With painstaking accuracy and satiny smoothness, He polishes away the dullness of our old life.

Farewell Familiar

The woman of Isaiah's account must turn away from the familiar prison walls and begin walking in another direction. In the same manner, if we cling to the dwelling place of the past, we cannot move toward our destiny. We must release the former housing situation and relocate to a new residence. The place we were dwelling was a dark, filthy, smelly, pest-infested dungeon. Negative and incorrect thought processes about our identity led us into dark places in our minds. Our thoughts were dripping with nagging negativity, crawling with pests of inferiority and insecurity, and reeking with a deficient sense of value and understated worth.

Standing on the outside of the prison walls, we are ready to make the full conversion from fearfulness to faithfulness, from powerless to powerful, from out-of-control thoughts to self-control, and from hopelessness to filled with hope in Christ.

We have made the exchange from ill-fitted, faded, soiled, and tattered clothing to donning the strong vestments of faith, power, authority, and self-control. The adornment of encouragement now cloaks our shoulders and wraps our thoughts. We have drenched our lips with everlasting water at the fountain of life and infused them with colors of the bejeweled robe of praise.

There is a promise fulfilled to accompany our new garments. Isaiah said to our daughter of Zion, "*The uncircumcised and defiled will not enter you again.*" (Isa. 52:1b) This statement confirms it is possible to have a completely new lifestyle which prevents the former ways from returning.

The Great Exchange

The apostle Paul taught the Romans how to convert from their old patterns into a new way of living, as he taught of

Christ being their focus and the center of their lives. Paul spoke of complete transformation when he said, "And do not be conformed to this world, but be transformed by the renewing of your mind, so that you may prove what the will of God is, that which is good and acceptable and perfect" (Rom. 12:1-2 NASB).

What Paul taught the Romans applies to God's people today. This conversion is a result of centering our lives on Jesus and being full of His presence through the indwelling of the Holy Spirit. Paul taught that our way of life and our daily routine can morph into something we desire as a direct result of changing how we think and changing our mind (our leb, the essence of who we are).

In recent research about the neuroplasticity of the human brain, scientists have learned that thoughts have organic components which can be measured. While conducting various brain scans on people, researchers prompted the thoughts of the participants and discovered there is a measurable difference in the type of activity that occurs in the brain between negative and positive thoughts.

Neuroplasticity is the "ability of the brain to form and reorganize synaptic connection, especially in response to learning or following an injury."[10] In other words, neuroplasticity describes how the brain changes over time. Please note the word *reorganize* in the definition of neuroplasticity. The human brain can reorganize itself by forming neural connections throughout life. Neuroplasticity allows the neurons (nerve cells) in the brain to compensate for injury and disease and to adjust their activities in response to new situations or changes in their environment. The mind can change and reorganize throughout our lifetime.

The study of neuroplasticity both affirms and confirms what the apostle Paul taught more than two thousand years ago. He explained to the Romans and Philippians that the mind could indeed undergo willfully directed transformation.

It can be changed, spiritually speaking, as well as physically, when we put the right thoughts to work in our brains.

Understanding that neuroplasticity of the brain means the brain itself compensates for injury and disease also reveals another scientific confirmation of the truth about God's redemptive work. In the sacrifice of Jesus as the Lamb slain for all humanity, God's redemptive work supplied for healing. Isaiah, who lived approximately seven hundred years before Jesus' birth, prophesied about the imminent arrival of the Messiah, whom we now know is Jesus. Isaiah's prophecy declared healing would come through the suffering of this forthcoming Messiah.

> Surely he took up our pain and bore our suffering, yet we considered him punished by God, stricken by him, and afflicted. But he was pierced for our transgressions, he was crushed for our iniquities; the punishment that brought us peace was on him, and by his wounds we are healed. (Isaiah 53:4-5)

When the apostle Peter—a disciple who was chosen by Jesus, who walked with Him throughout His ministry, witnessed His crucifixion and resurrection, was in the upper room at the arrival of the Holy Spirit, and then made his life focus to preach and teach the Gospel of Jesus Christ—spoke of Jesus' healing, he said, "He Himself bore our sins in His body on the tree, that we might die to sin and live to righteousness. By His wounds you have been healed." (1 Pet. 2:24 ESV)

Jesus, the Christ, the Messiah, was born and lived as prophesied by Isaiah. The Messiah performed His acts of ministry and teaching, was ministered to, bore the sorrow of our punishment, then died—just as prophesied by Isaiah. Peter witnessed the life and death of Jesus Christ. Peter was also privileged to witness the resurrected Jesus and to see Him transfigured into Heaven. Jesus is now at the right hand of

God the Father (1 Pet. 3:22) making intercession on behalf of His followers (Rom. 8:34).[11] Therefore, Peter spoke of our healing through Jesus in the past tense, that the work of healing had already been accomplished by Jesus' suffering and death on the cross.

Both Isaiah and Peter spoke to the truth that Christ's suffering and death provided for our healing—physical, emotional, and spiritual. To know this healing, we must place our faith in the Lord and allow Him to bring His healing to us. We must make a great exchange. That is, we collect what is right and true about ourselves and our relationship to God in Christ. Then we convert that into our transformed life.

Making Ribbons from Chains

We are making the conversion from being chained to the negative issues of past events in our life to willingly tying ourselves—with the silken soft ribbons of God's love, grace, and mercy—to the positive flow of the healing river of life that comes from Jesus Christ, through His Spirit dwelling within us.

Behold, I make all things new.
(Revelation 21:5 NIV)

The way to make this conversion is through our thought life. We know what garments to wear—faith, power, choice, authority, self-control, strength, encouragement, right communication, and praise. Each of these garments requires stretching for them to be ever-fitting. We must exercise our *faith* in God so that it will grow. That means we must reach beyond where we are comfortable and trust the Lord to guide us as we navigate our way through that uncomfortable place. When we stretch our reach, our faith will grow. We will become more confident in God—placing us in the exact position, at the precise moment in time, to fulfill His purpose in us—even when it is uncomfortable. With greater confidence in our identity in the Lord, we will increase in our ability to walk in the *power* and *authority* we possess through Jesus Christ. Consciously choosing to exercise *self-control* in every situation allows us to be intentional in every area of life.

The culmination of growing our faith, wielding our power and authority through the Word and Christ, and walking in self-control aids us in encouraging others in their walk. Through all these things, we will be speaking life into our situations, as well as speaking life into others' lives. Praise will be the natural overflow, and we will find we praise God more often, more fervently, and more effectively for all He is doing in us and through us.

This growing faith begins the cycle of positive, Christ-centered thought. This thought cycle is identical to the negative thought cycle, with one exception—the thoughts are opposite. The Christ-centered thought cycle begins with a positive, Christ-centered thought and continues when we expel and give voice to those thoughts in the form of words. Our words touch the atmosphere. We hear our own words bouncing back to us. Those words go directly back into our soul. Then the cycle repeats and grows in intensity. In the same way that harmful speech affects others, when we speak positive, Christ-centered words to another person, we positively affect their thoughts, their mind, their soul, and their opinion. With each Christ-centered statement, we intensify and grow right thinking toward our self, and we continue to grow in understanding our value.

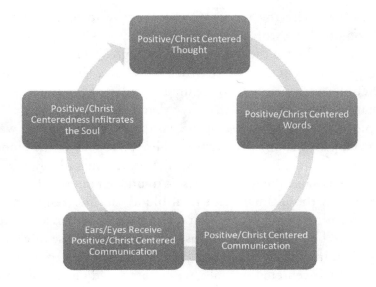

The indwelling presence of the Holy Spirit encourages our cycle of thought. He walks with us, always. Jesus, while speaking to His disciples, said he would not abandon His followers. He sent His presence to dwell with us by His spirit (John 14:16-18). In the Old and New Testaments, we read that God will never leave us, nor forsake us (Deut. 31:6; Heb. 13:5). When we dwell with Him, God fulfills His Word and provides shelter for us in His nest, under His wings, softly covered by His feathers (Ps. 91:1-4).

As we learn to put on and utilize our new garments, to think new positive, Christ-centered thoughts, we are enabled to understand and walk in the truth that God is worthy of praise wherever life's issues may be—as they run the gamut from fabulous, to okay, to less than stellar, to devastating. Even when subjected to the outrageous, sinful behavior of someone else, God is still good. When we have shattered promising opportunities through our own poor choices, mistakes, and immoral behavior, God is always kind, loving, merciful, and compassionate toward us. God is worthy to receive praise through all the storms we must weather.

The author of the book of Hebrews agreed with this choice to praise, no matter what, when he wrote, "Through Him then, let us continually offer up a sacrifice of praise to God, that is, the fruit of lips that give thanks to His name" (Heb. 13:15 NASB). In his use of the word *sacrifice*, the writer was drawing an analogy. The writer of Hebrews spoke of the blood sacrifices offered as an outward sign under the old covenant. In this passage, the writer wants us to understand that because Jesus was the ultimate and final blood sacrifice required in establishing the new covenant, our inward obedience is now revealed by the fruit of our lips becoming our praise offering.

Making the conversion from negative self-talk to positive and Christ-centered self-talk, we choose to rid our mind from the cancer of distressing words, which includes snares and entrapment of our own making, uncertainty, doubt, discord, strife, contention, and conflict.

Our new collection allows us to replace these damaging amalgamations of fools' gold of the mind. The distasteful toxic thoughts exchanged, we now sip with delight, swallowing the amber, honey-like sweetness of kind words (Prov. 16:24). We smile at the tickle of effervescent joy from the bubbling brook of wisdom (Prov. 18:4). We drink our boundless fill of the endless flow of knowledge, righteousness, and understanding from the fountain of life (Prov. 10:11; 13:14; 16:22).

As we alter the poorly designed apparel of incorrect thinking to our new, personally tailored wear of correct thinking, we will unearth the revelation of our uniquely designed, God-given purpose.

Glimmers of the Crown

The Great Exchange

Do not be conformed to this world but be transformed by the renewing of your minds, so that you may prove what the will of God is, that which is good and acceptable and perfect. (Rom. 12:2 NIV)

I waited patiently for the Lord; and He inclined to me and heard my cry. He brought me up out of the pit of destruction, out of the miry clay, and He set my feet upon a rock making my footsteps firm. He put a new song in my mouth, a song of praise to our God; Many will see and fear and will trust in the Lord. (Ps. 40:1-3 NASB)

PART 5

Connect

Sit enthroned

CHAPTER 8

Clarity and Sparkle

As we have seen in our preparation for your royal rendez-vous, a gemstone mined from the earth is not left in its rough form. The stonecutter must exercise a tedious, intricate process to make the conversion from raw to brilliant. With each change, the value of the stone increases. The jewel begins as nothing more than stone hewn from the side of a cave; the crusty edges sawn, and the undesirable chunks are ground further down, leaving only tiny microscopic grains. The grainy edges are then sanded, and facets beveled, revealing the true worth and value of the gemstone.

Ashen Heap to Brilliance

When a lapidary puts a gemstone on the wheel, he creates friction with sand. The force of the sand against the spinning stone produces heat to burn away the unwanted particles, resulting in little mounds of ashen stone forming on the table.

Ashes come from times of fire. There are, and will continue to be, times we experience fiery trials in life. When this happens, the garbage of our lives gets burned away, but we are left to experience the joy of being rescued. We are not spared the trial, nor are we afforded reprieve from the heat of the flame. The only way to get ashes is for something to burn.

We want the Lord to burn away those things in our lives that hinder us from walking in our destiny and fulfilling our purpose. We want the Lord to reveal to us what we need to sacrifice on the altar for our own sake, as well as for the sake of our relationship with Him. We will mourn the things we must sacrifice—even those dysfunctional hang-ups to which we have become so accustomed and emotionally attached. Suffering through the pain of change, we grieve the time of relinquishing to the fire the old, ill-fitting but comfortable, mindsets. When we submit to His authority, place upon the altar these incorrect mindsets and allow them to burn away, in their place we receive His beautiful mercy and grace. The Lord promises beauty for the ashes of our suffering. He promises the oil of joy in place of our sorrow, mourning, and grief. Our lowered face of despair will be lifted to bring festive praise. Isaiah revealed this promise when he said, "To all who mourn in Israel, he will give a crown of beauty for ashes, a joyous blessing instead of mourning, festive praise instead of despair." (Isa. 61:3a)

As you continue to work through this process, you may wonder how or why these Scriptures of the Old Testament would, or could, apply to your modern life. After all, we live in the twenty-first century, and Isaiah lived and recorded events about seven hundred years before Jesus was born—nearly three thousand years ago. Not only that, you may think, *Isaiah's prophecies and accounts were written to the Israelites, God's chosen people, so how could that apply to me?*

Paul addressed this dilemma in his letters because the people to whom he ministered (two thousand years ago) had the same question. To the church at Ephesus, Paul explained the choice God made to bring Gentiles, all people who were not born of Abraham's bloodline, into His family, the Israelites. Paul spoke of God's choice to join Gentiles into his family by adoption, as follows.

> Even before he made the world, God loved us and chose us in Christ to be holy and without fault in his eyes. God decided in advance to adopt us into his own family by bringing us to himself through Jesus Christ. This is what he wanted to do, and it gave him great pleasure. So we praise God for the glorious grace he has poured out on us who belong to his dear Son. He is so rich in kindness and grace that he purchased our freedom with the blood of his Son and forgave our sins. He has showered his kindness on us, along with all wisdom and understanding. (Eph. 1:4-8)

Because of the life, death, burial, and resurrection of Jesus, God has adopted *all* those who place their trust in Him, through Jesus, into His family.

Paul expanded the explanation of the concept of Gentiles being adopted into God's family (the Israelites, Abraham's bloodline), clarifying there was no distinction in our heirship when he wrote to the church at Galatia.

> ...those who have faith are children of Abraham. God would justify the Gentiles by faith...so those who rely on faith are blessed along with Abraham, the man of faith...He redeemed us in order that the blessing given to Abraham might come to the Gentiles in Christ Jesus, so that by faith we might receive the promise of the Spirit... So in Christ Jesus you are all children of God through faith, for all of you who were baptized into Christ have clothed yourselves with Christ. There is neither Jew nor

Gentile, neither slave nor free, nor is there male and female, for you are all one in Christ Jesus. *If you belong to Christ, then you are Abraham's seed, and heirs according to the promise.* (Gal. 3:7-9, 14, 26-29, author's emphasis)

Jesus was born through the bloodline of Abraham, as we are shown in the gospel of Matthew, as well as the Gospel of Luke.[12] Placing our faith in Jesus, the Christ, who purchased and redeemed us by His shed blood on the cross, makes us sons and daughters of The Most High God, and joint heirs with Jesus Christ.

Because we belong to God's family, in Christ, we (Gentiles) should heed the words spoken by the Lord through His prophets and be ready to receive the promises, as well. The prophet, Isaiah, said we rise out of the ashes of our past, put on a beautiful crown, are filled with praise, experience the blessing of joy, and are seated in our God-purposed position.

It is time to take our last step, out of the ashes, to shine with His brilliance.

Glimmers of the Crown

For no matter how many promises God has made, they are "Yes" in Christ. And so through Him the "Amen" is spoken by us to the glory of God. Now it is God who makes both us and you stand firm in Christ. He anointed us, set His seal of ownership on us, and put His Spirit in our hearts as a deposit, guaranteeing what is to come. (2 Cor. 1:20-22)

CHAPTER 9

Your Royal Rendezvous

On this journey of exploration, excavation, and transformation, we have broken through barricades to mine the gems of spiritual and personal success. We identified old mindsets, excavated them, and then toppled them, defeating their tyranny on our life. With the meticulous skill of a world-class gem cutter, we revamped our thoughts, and triggered a metamorphosis of heart and mind. We are wearing our new garments of splendorous faith and power, and we hold the scepter bejeweled with choice, authority, and control. The royal robe of strength drapes across our shoulders and our lips are moistened and healed as we drink from the fountain of life. It is time to make the rendezvous for which we have been preparing.

The Point

Every gemstone is sourced from earth's materials being forged together over time and fixed into a crystallized form. As the lapidary removes the rough, it reveals the shape of the stone, and the artisan envisions the stone's potential final form. Each gemstone, whatever the final shape and cut, has the same parts—a table, a crown, a girdle, a pavilion, and a cutlet. The cutlet is the junction where the facets meet, light connects to each intersection, and then refracts and bends through the gem, thus creating its radiance. This tip at the bottom—the cutlet—is the foundation for the beauty displayed at the top and crown.

Even when individual gems possess the same style cut—round, oval, princess, emerald, or marquise—the crystal formation is unique to each stone and lends itself to a specific shape. In the same way, people have many shared similarities. We are all designed by the Creator with similar materials—skin, blood, skeleton, and nerves—making us considerably like one another. Yet, like precious jewels we are all forged by the fluctuation of our life experiences and crystallized uniquely as a result of the circumstances. We live our days with the reality and sameness of our humanity. In our alikeness, we each have birth, life experiences, and death. Still, each of us is unique in personality, gifts, our specific life events, and our response to them. As we have learned and discussed throughout this book, our perspective is developed significantly through experiences, both negative and positive. Thus, many of us, along with celebrating life's joys, have nurtured dysfunction throughout our lives that must be halted to achieve our fullest potential. Together, we have CONFRONTED those issues, worked toward their COLLAPSE, COLLECTED the right information about ourselves, and CONVERTED our thinking. It is time to bring those together and make the endpoint connection.

Promenade

As though ascending the stairs of a palace entry, we step through the doorway and begin the promenade to our anticipated destination, the throne room. In this phase of our journey, we set the rendezvous point and arrange for our meeting.

Your royal rendezvous—and mine—is a scheduled meeting in a specific place, at a specified time, with the One who is the King of all kings. Jehovah God is the greatest of royalty. This King of the Universe, the Designer of all creation and Creator of you and me, desires to commune with His creation. He bids us come near to Him and enter His throne room. Our invitation is inked with the blood of the sacrifice given to reconcile all people back to a relationship with God. When we accept God's invitation, we enter His presence through the veil of the blood of Jesus, His Son, and bow ourselves before the throne of grace, where we are also recognized as His child.

Specific Place

In Matthew's account of the Gospel, he offers the description of Jesus' teaching about communicating with God. Matthew quotes Jesus, saying,

> When you pray, you are not to be like the hypocrites; for they love to stand and pray in the synagogues and on the street corners so that they may be seen by men. Truly I say to you, they have their reward in full. But you, when you pray, go into your inner room, close your door and pray to your Father who is in secret, and your Father who sees what is done in secret will reward you. And when you are praying, do not use meaningless repetition as the Gentiles do, for they suppose that they

will be heard for their many words. So, do not be like them; for your Father knows what you need before you ask Him. (Matt. 6:5-8 NASB)

Jesus begins His instruction by contrasting the two approaches of communicating with God, starting with the wrong method. He describes a person behaving like an actor in a play, performing for the notice, recognition, and applause of people. Jesus used the Greek word *hypocrite* or *hupokrinomai*, which means an actor, one who wears a mask, or a person who invents a certain demeanor, but their real character is different than that which is portrayed.[13,14] Jesus stressed that communing with God is not for the benefit of being seen and noticed by other people. Instead, Jesus emphasized that the purpose of this interaction between a person and God is to be seen and known by God.

Continuing His teaching, Jesus addresses the importance of where to meet and communicate with God. He describes a specific kind of place saying, "go into your inner room" (Matt. 6:6 NASB). The Greek word for room in this passage is *tameion*,[15] which means an interior room without doors or windows to the outside, such as a pantry, or a secret storage room in one's house. With this visualization of a small interior space, we understand Jesus was describing a closed-off area disconnected from all the other activities of the household.

In modern cultures (and depending on the region of the world in which we live), the way houses are constructed varies regarding the number and types of rooms. Nevertheless, Jesus shows us that our rendezvous location should be strategically selected to be a quiet place where there is little opportunity for interruption and distraction. Whatever room or area that is available to us, our rendezvous point should be a positive place for us. It needs to occur in a place we eagerly anticipate being, an area we like and enjoy. My rendezvous point is in a small den area of my house. This den is not connected to the busier living room and kitchen. I like being in the den and look forward to each appointment.

Situated near the south windows in the den is a big, soft, overstuffed chair that serves as my designated meeting site. There is familiarity to the location because this chair and I have history—twenty years to be exact. When I initially purchased the chair, I was redecorating our home. We had purchased the house from another family and had lived in it for about two years. We had budgeted some money to make a few improvements and started with the master bedroom. This chair was an accent piece, complementing our walls and bedding with its light, buttery yellow canvas splashed with a floral print and trimmed with blue denim piping. When I gaze at its sunny colors, a chord of cheerful emotion rings in my soul.

The chair began its time in our house as a decorative item. While our children were still living at home, rarely did I have an opportunity to go into my bedroom simply to sit. In those years, by the time I completed my last task to finish out the day and prep for the next one, everyone else had been asleep for at least two hours. So, I would traipse into the bedroom and slink into my pajamas, then fall headfirst into bed knowing that in only six short hours it would all begin again. As the children got older and I was alone at home during the morning hours, this chair, illuminated and warmed by the south sunshine, became my preferred resting spot. More importantly, this peaceful, happy setting quickly became my designated location for communing with the Lord through Bible reading and prayer. My insatiable hunger for the Word led me to this place daily to satisfy my spiritual appetite. Many days I found myself curled into this chair, immersed in the Scriptures with a notepad and pen, balancing reference books on its rolled arms and delving into carefully stacked commentaries.

Eventually, I repurposed a bedroom into a den with a study area and relocated the chair to that room. It served as the perfect backdrop for me to bow low and kneel at the throne of grace.

Specific Time

When a sovereign takes the throne to entertain visitors they do so only at specified times. Under the old covenant, during the time of the tabernacle in the wilderness and the days of the Temple, the Lord made Himself available for visitation at specified times in the Holy of Holies. After Jesus offered Himself as the ultimate sacrifice, there was no longer a barrier to prevent people from approaching God. The Sovereign Lord took His throne to make Himself available to us at all times.

Throughout the Scriptures, we are instructed to call upon God. Isaiah said to, "Seek the Lord while he may be found; call on him while he is near" (Isa. 55:6). James bids, "Come near to God and he will come near to you" (James 4:8), and explains, "The prayer of a righteous person is powerful and effective" (James 5:16b). The author of Hebrews invites, "Let us then approach God's throne of grace with confidence, so that we may receive mercy and find grace to help us in our time of need" (Heb. 4:16).

In this new covenant, when we receive the gift of reconciliation to God through Jesus, our heart becomes His temple, and He gives us the opportunity to choose when we approach Him. God is seated on His throne awaiting our arrival. Setting a specific time can be challenging. Every season of life presents its own set of obstacles to the calendar.

When my children were younger, my days were filled with chubby hugs, diaper changes, bottles, unexplained cries, cleaning up spills and random messes, picking up toys, cooking, cleaning, laundry, ironing, more laundry, and more cleaning. I longed for special time with the Lord, but the only moments available for solitude and quiet contemplation were at about one or two o'clock in the morning. So, after I completed my tasks and the house was quiet and dark, with my family soundly asleep, I would roll out of bed and pick up my Bible from the nightstand. Stealthily, as if on cat feet, I stepped softly across the bedroom and into the master bathroom. I shut the door before turning on the light, wrapped up in a fluffy robe, and laid myself across the floor to read and pray.

Those nights opened my heart to truths in the Word of God as I had never experienced. The growth in my relationship with the Lord helped me cope more effectively as a young wife and mother. Those nights of pursuing God's presence in prayer and immersing myself in the Word resonate in my heart and mind, helping me with life issues today. I rest in the assurance that at the precise moment of need, I will continue to be reminded of the sacred Scriptures learned during those late nights of pursuing the Lord.

While late-night hours were the most opportune times for this rendezvous when my children were small, schedules changed as they grew, and I began working more often outside the home. Therefore, my daily appointment with The King moved further around the clock to 4:30 a.m. I enjoy praying with the dark skies of pre-dawn, and it is exhilarating to celebrate the Lord's nearness as I watch the sun peel away the deep indigo into royal. I see the sky swell into brilliant orange, then bright golden daybreak. My scheduled appointment time has remained consistent for many years to step into this beloved place for uninterrupted time with the most cherished One who calls me His treasure.

If this concept is new to you, begin by setting aside a block of time—twenty to thirty minutes—when you might typically watch television, read, or engage in some other activity. Do this until it becomes a habit. That means put it in your calendar, and don't mark over it with something else. You will need to do it at the same time every day. Much of the research shows that to form a new habit, we must repeat the same action, identically, fifteen to twenty-one times. Therefore, to set your royal rendezvous, schedule it twenty-one days in a row, at the same time, and do not allow anything else to interfere with it. Following this schedule change will accomplish two things. First, you will remove a nonessential item from your calendar. Secondly, you will replace that nonessential with a positive, life-transforming practice that empowers you to conquer those things lurking in the shadows of your mind.

Throne Room—Battleground

The third element of a military rendezvous is to determine a strategy for the battle to overcome the enemy. In our royal rendezvous, we are seeking victory in every facet of life over the adversary of our souls, who is Satan. We need to remind ourselves that Satan is a liar and the father of all lies. We know this because Jesus described this adversary in absolute terms when He said, "He was a murderer from the beginning, and does not stand in the truth because there is no truth in him. When he lies, he speaks what is natural to him, for he is a liar and the father of lies and half-truths" (John 8:44 AMP). Jesus also taught that our adversary's goal is to steal, kill, and destroy (John 10:10), and he will use every method and channel at his disposal to accomplish his mission. He wants to steal our peace, kill our joy, and destroy us from the inside. As we have discussed throughout this book, Satan's primary method to bring about our inner destruction is to use the lies we have received, believed, and internalized about ourselves at various times in our lives. He wants us to think we are so botched and spoiled that we are permanently ruined and not worthy of being loved—particularly not worthy of being loved by God. Satan will throw these lies and memories into our thoughts while we are praying, and we will have to fight against the negative thoughts and overcome them with the Truth. That is why I refer to our time before the throne of grace as time on the battleground.

Therefore, we must focus on the truth about God, who He is, and who we are in Him through Jesus Christ (For a list of these truths, refer to *What the Bible Reveals About God* and *What the Bible Reveals About Who We Are to God in Christ* in Chapter 6). God revealed that His love for us is so immense, He presented the only perfect sacrifice to offer us redemption and reconciliation into right relationship with Him. "For God so loved the world, that he gave his only Son, that whoever believes in him should not perish but have eternal life" (John 3:16 ESV). I say that is extraordinary love.

The plan has been laid out for us, and it is our responsibility to execute it to achieve victory. The winning strategy requires our response to the Lord's beckoning us to spend time with Him and in His Word.

We have learned that Jesus taught us to approach God with a humble heart and to reserve for Him a designated place and time. He also trained His followers on how to speak to God, that is, to pray. In Jesus' example, found in the Gospel accounts of Matthew and Luke, and commonly referred to as The Lord's Prayer, He began with an instruction. When Jesus said, "Pray, then, in this way" (Matt. 6:9), He was coaching all those who want to be like Him how to entreat God, who is our Father and King. While it is good to memorize Scripture, we need to understand that Jesus did not tell us to repeat His exact words mindlessly, but to follow His example of how to pray. Learning from Jesus' example of speaking with the Father, we will refer to Matthew 6:9-13 from *The Amplified Bible* to note the essential elements of communication with God, which are as follows.

1. Offer worship, praise, adoration, and honor, recognizing God for who He is—"Our Father, who is in heaven, Hallowed be Your name."

2. Pursue the will of God—"Your kingdom come, Your will be done On earth as it is in heaven."

3. Confession and Repentance—marked by a remorseful heart over our sinfulness—"And forgive us our debts, as we have forgiven our debtors [letting go of both the wrong and the resentment]."

4. Petition—asking with boldness because of our confidence in His ability to answer

    a. Provision for our essential needs—"Give us this day our daily bread."

    b. Protection from succumbing to evil—"And do not lead us into temptation"

    c. Problems specific to my life that need solutions—"but deliver us from evil."

5. Worship, praise, adoration, and honor, again recognizing God as the Sovereign Creator who is worthy of all glory, marked with continued thanksgiving for what He has already done for us, and for what He will do in us, for us, and through us—"For Yours is the kingdom and the power and the glory forever. Amen."

We approach God's throne boldly, as the writer of Hebrews directed (Heb. 4:16), because of our relationship with Him through Jesus. Still, we must enter the throne room humbly because we know we need mercy, and we are unworthy to enter God's presence without Jesus.

Battle Gear

In this war waged in the spirit realm, we need to be clothed with all the armor essential to fighting for victory. Paul, in his letter to the Ephesians, describes the kind of battle we engage in as hand-to-hand combat, yet "...not against flesh and blood, but against the rulers, against the authorities, against the powers of this dark world and against the spiritual forces of evil in the heavenly realms" (Eph. 6:12). Paul then lists the armor we need, naming each piece: belt of truth, breastplate of righteousness, shoes of the gospel of peace, shield of faith, helmet of salvation, and sword of the spirit (Eph. 6:10-17). Each of these items is designed for a specific protective covering, and as a full suit of armor, they work together, guarding us against the enemy's attacks on our soul. The Lord provides this armor, but we must clothe ourselves with it.

Paul names each piece of armor in the order that a Roman soldier would suit up for battle. Our vital organs, particularly the heart, are protected by the body armor of the breastplate of righteousness and belted with truth. The truth and righteousness of who Jesus is and our righteousness because of who we are in Him enable us to walk in truth and integrity. We wear this breastplate, knowing we are made righteous through the blood of Jesus, and He and His righteousness within us protects our hearts. With the shoes of the gospel of peace, we walk sure-footed over the work of the enemy meant to trip us and make us stumble. The shield of faith is the moveable piece of armor that we hold to thwart whatever comes against us, turning it in the direction from which the attack comes. Circumstances of life are difficult at times, and when that happens, the enemy of our souls will use the fiery darts of those times to attempt to destroy us. When we hold up our faith in the Lord (the shield) and stand firm with it, those arrows cannot penetrate. The helmet of salvation protects the mind that contains the knowledge of our position with the Lord. When feelings of overwhelm come—and they will—our mind is protected, and we can stand firm in the knowledge that we are saved by the redemptive blood of Jesus that was shed on our behalf to reconcile us to God.

The final piece of armor is the only weapon of offense, the sword of the spirit, which is the Word of God. When we go into battle at the throne of grace, we battle best when we brandish the sword of the Word of God. We employ this weapon by calling out Scripture in prayer. We do this to put it on the front line because we know God is true to His Word and speaking Scripture will strengthen our spirit. The Lord tells us through Isaiah that His word never returns empty-handed, but always brings back a harvest. "So will My word be which goes out of My mouth; It will not return to Me void [useless, without result], Without accomplishing what I desire, And without succeeding in the matter for which I sent it" (Isa. 55:11 AMP).

Now, I know many may read this and believe they don't know enough Bible verse to pray the Scriptures. None of us is born with that knowledge, so we must feed it to ourselves by creating the habit of reading the Word and meditating on it. The writer of Hebrews stated,

> For the word of God is living and active and full of power [making it operative, energizing, and effective]. It is sharper than any two-edged sword, penetrating as far as the division of the soul and spirit [the completeness of a person], and of both joints and marrow [the deepest parts of our nature], exposing and judging the very thoughts and intentions of the heart. (Heb. 4:12 AMP)

I am living proof that as we rendezvous daily with the Lord, petition Him, seek to know Him and pursue our relationship with Him by spending specific time in prayer and reading the Bible, we will learn His Word and become more acquainted with Him and the Scriptures.

This living Word of God reveals our true self to us and causes us to come to terms with our brokenness. These revelations trigger our confessing to God those sins and issues that beset and weigh us down, our seeking the Lord's forgiveness of them, and repenting—fully turning away—from them. Every time we pour the Word into our mind and heart, we will grow in our walk with the Lord. As we grow, we desire more growth, which leads to more Bible reading, increased time in prayer, a better understanding of our armor, and the ability to wage war in the spirit realm more effectively.

At the Foot of the Cross

Without the facets of a gemstone merging at the point, the light would not connect in the best way to exhibit the gem's crystallized brilliance. In the same way, the convergence point for each of us is the foundation of our mindset.

When Jesus was crucified, the first reference to the Messiah in Scripture was fulfilled. When Adam and Eve were cast out of the Garden of Eden because of their sin, God pronounced a judgment and spoke a prophetic statement about His redemptive plan when He said, "And I will put enmity between you and the woman, and between your offspring and her offspring; He will bruise and tread your head underfoot, and you will lie in wait and bruise His heel" (Gen. 3:15 AMPC). The significance of this declaration is in the feet because feet represent authority. When a king sat enthroned, everyone in his presence was placed at a level lower than the foot of the throne, symbolizing that all the king's subjects were under his authority. Additionally, when a king would conquer an enemy, often he would stand with his foot on the neck of the ruler of the rival nation as a show of his victory and authority over both that ruler and nation. In this case, God is explicitly speaking of the feet of the Messiah, Jesus, and that He would defeat Satan.

When Jesus was crucified, His heels were bruised, and He crushed the head of Satan by His resurrection from the dead, thereby defeating death, Hell, and the grave (1 Cor. 15). The fulfillment of God's Word is realized when He bestowed upon Jesus all authority in Heaven and on earth. Paul refers to this fulfillment of Scripture when he quotes from Psalm 8:6 in his letters to the Ephesians and the Corinthians. "And

He put all things under His feet and gave Him to be head over all things to the church" (Eph. 1:22 NKJV), and "For he has put everything under his feet." (1 Cor. 15:27a). Jesus also conferred upon all His disciples (those who want to be like their teacher) the authority to cast out evil spirits, to bring healing of every kind of disease and sickness, as well as preach the Gospel. That means that you and I also have the authority to break and remove the chains that bind our past to today (Matt. 10). In mining, the "principal vein or source of the region, or [the] principal source of supply," is called the mother lode.[16] When someone claims to have hit the mother lode, they mean they have acquired a valuable treasure. In our case, the mother lode is the cross of Christ. It is deliverance from our sin and shame, the liberty to walk in holiness, and the source of our treasured freedom.

To see the crowning glory for which our hearts long, we must have the right foundation, which is the mindset centered upon the cross of Christ. A crown must balance on the head of the royal. Therefore, we must rest in the balance of our identity with the King of Kings, humbling ourselves at the foot of the cross and submitting to Jesus' authority, before we can be crowned at the throne of grace.

Glimmers of the Crown

Jesus' feet represent authority. Our feet represent the foundation of our lives and the authority bestowed to us from the Lord. As we walk with the Lord and delight in His counsel, we will find the path He has laid before us, and we will prosper in our endeavors.

How lovely on the mountains
Are the feet of him who brings good news,
Who announces peace
And brings good news of happiness,
Who announces salvation,
And says to Zion, "Your God reigns!"
(Isa. 52:7-8 NASB)

My steps have held fast to Your paths. My feet have not slipped.
(Ps. 17:5 NASB)

The law of his God is in his heart; His steps do not slip.
(Ps. 37:31 NASB)

How blessed is the man who does not walk in the counsel of the wicked,
Nor stand in the path of sinners,
Nor sit in the seat of scoffers!
But his delight is in the law of the Lord,
And in His law he meditates day and night.
He will be like a tree firmly planted by streams of water,
Which yields its fruit in its season
And its leaf does not wither;
And in whatever he does, he prospers.
(Ps. 1:1-3 NASB)

CHAPTER 10

Take Your Rightful Place—Step Into Your Purpose

O ur daughter of Zion received the paramount directive when she was commanded to take her rightful place as an heir to the crown and its accompanying authority. Like this daughter, God formed each of us as an exclusive package of physique, personality, talents, and gifts, and called every one of us a masterpiece of His making (Ps. 139; Eph. 2:10). With that, God has reserved a specific place in His kingdom to be fulfilled by each uniquely formed person. To access our reservation, we must accept the gift of salvation through Jesus Christ and do what He commands—love God with all our heart, soul, mind, and strength, and love other people in the same way we love our self (Acts 4:12; Matt. 22:34-40). Amazingly, God knows us intimately, with all our faults and failures, yet He chooses to love us and reconcile us to Himself. Through Jesus, He provided the way for us to take our rightful place and fulfill our purpose in His kingdom. He has given us a position of authority over our past and the enemy of our souls. Together, these facets unite to create the brilliance of our crown, and we can rise as children of the King and take our rightful place at the throne of grace.

Glorious Connection

Here is where it all comes together. We have confronted and collapsed the obstacles to our success inside the essence of our self. We have collected the right information concerning ourselves, and made the conversion from old, ineffective mindsets to a fresh, life-giving outlook. As we adorn our lives with these jewels, making application of our newfound understanding, we come to the final raiment, the crown for which we have awaited: life connection.

Do you remember at the beginning of this journey when we crawled deep into the cave, searching for those things blocking our spirit, and preventing our ability to succeed? We began chipping away at the rough, encrusted stone. It was the fools' gold veneer we had so carefully wrapped around our heart with hope that no one would see the flaws behind our shiny façade. As the Holy Spirit revealed the identity of that crust, we felt the burden of its heaviness on our life. We struck intentional blows to break it down, and as shards of the past fell away, something valuable began to appear.

The Holy Spirit's revelation exposed our cover, but He did not leave us in that overwhelmingly shameful state. He tenderly turned on the search lamp inside the recesses of our mind. He helped us explore the deep crevices and fractures of our innermost being. He strengthened us to look at them, to see them fully for what they were. The Lord of Love gave us courage, and the words to stand up, confront, and say goodbye forever to those beastly notions.

With a cleansed heart and clear mind, we began refilling our essence, collecting the right thoughts, growing in our understanding about God, and grasping that our relationship to Him defines our identity through Jesus Christ. As we entrust our complete self to Him, the renewing of everything transforms us. Paul helps us understand about being remade into a new creation when he wrote, "Therefore if anyone is in Christ [that is, grafted in, joined to Him by faith in Him as Savior], he is a new creature [reborn and renewed by the Holy Spirit]; the old things [the previous moral and spiritual condition] have passed away. Behold, new things have come [because spiritual awakening brings a new life]" (2 Cor. 5:17 AMP). Paul is teaching us that the essence of who we are changes because we now identify with Jesus Christ. Our shame is removed by God's redemptive work on our behalf, through Jesus' death and resurrection. All the old is collapsed and gone, and all things become new.

Shining New Life

Let's take a moment to gaze at our reflection in the mirror and celebrate our new life. We are different. We have been washed clean, and we are continuously being cleansed as we walk in our faith. God is making us new. We are being transformed.

We can now move forward toward our life's vision, knowing who we are in Christ. Our life is no longer about our self-esteem. It is the realization that all our confidence and ability come from understanding our value in the Lord. The psalmist said, "God is the strength of my heart and my portion forever" (Ps. 73:26). We have collected the joy of the Lord in our spirits and are now connecting with life, strengthened with His joy (Neh. 8:10).

Rather than attempting merely to cover our past with a heavier façade of fools' gold or sweep it away and hide it and its accompanying shame, we have COLLAPSED the old way of thinking. We choose no longer to conform to old patterns that can lead to our devastation. Instead, we choose to be transformed into a new way that leads to succeeding in a life filled with peace and joy. We have decided to bring down a destructive, sinful thought life. We have chosen to be healed from old mindsets by replacing them with life-giving thoughts. We are now adorned with praise and adoration to God, who is making us new by His Holy Spirit.

We cannot allow the fear of changing to prevent us from moving forward. Stagnation will lead us back into old, dysfunctional patterns of thinking and behavior. Being different, renewed, and transformed by Jesus Christ will be what drives us toward spiritual and personal success.

My personal encounters with God began when I was playing in my backyard. At that moment, the Lord, through His Holy Spirit, revealed my need for Him, for His forgiveness, and His indwelling presence in me. Over the next three years, I developed my relationship with the Lord and learned to recognize His presence by pursuing Him in learning to read the Bible, pray, and discuss what I was learning. So, when He tugged at my heart in that first night of tabernacle at children's summer camp, I was assured it was the Lord calling me into His presence differently. He showed me during that week I could be different, set apart, and sanctified wholly in Him. Again, when seated in the balcony of the church listening to a missionary speaker, the Lord met me, and I recognized Him. That evening I had an unexpected revelation of His presence when He showed me a part of His plan and purpose for my life. In each instance, I was summoned to a royal rendezvous with the King of Kings, creator of the Universe.

Years later, I longed for some quiet, solitary time when my mind was fresh, and my spirit awakened to the Lord and what He wanted to show me. I wanted to be able to focus on Him and what He needed to correct in my life. I yearned for time to linger in His presence without distraction. So, I asked the Lord to please awaken me in the dark, early morning hours to spend time with Him. My wonderful God heard me and granted this request. Then, I added to my request that He would not only awaken me but that He would awaken me with a song in my heart for Him and His glory. Without fail, my kind, loving, and merciful Lord awakens me each morning sometime after 4:00, with a song of praise and worship in my heart to recognize His presence, to enter praise and worship of Him, and petition to Him without distraction.

The best news is that I am not special. The Bible reveals to us that God does not play favorites (Rom. 2:11; Acts 10:34). He does not have a favored child who receives more of His presence than another. Each person on this planet has the same opportunity I do to experience a royal rendezvous—every single day, with the Creator of the Universe, the One True and Living God.

We can never exhaust God's presence. He never runs out of His presence.

Crowning Jewel

At this rendezvous, we are crowned by God Himself, as His children. He crowns us with His righteousness. He crowns us with the greatest value of all—the crown of life we obtain through the shed blood of Jesus. You see, redemption is all about God paying the ransom for our return to Himself. God created people because He desired a loving family, one filled with love for Him and one another as He loves us.

God is not a selfish, narcissistic being who sits in the heavens and thinks up ways to prove His narcissism. Jehovah God is the Great I AM. He is The One who created each of us to be loved by Him and return love to Him. John repeats

Jesus' command when he tells us to love one another because love originates from God, so everyone who loves God and knows God can love God and love others of God's creation. John goes on to say that if we do not love one another, then we do not know God. Why does John say that? Because he also explains that God is love (1 John 4:7-8).

Love is not an attribute of God. Love is the very essence of who God is. Because of His love, He is also jealous about us. That does not mean He is jealous of us. God created me and all other individuals who have ever lived or will ever live. Therefore, what could you or I possibly possess that God would be jealous of? The answer is, absolutely nothing. God is God, you are not, and I am not. I cannot call anything into existence that He does not allow. God has no reason of any sort to be jealous of His creation. He is jealous about us like a doting father over his children or as a protective husband would be for his cherished bride. This magnificent God wants us to have a right relationship with Himself, to understand His greatness and awesome power, as well as His intimate knowledge of us. He desires us to be filled with His goodness, and to know, experience, and enjoy His presence without interruption. Because we are His finite creations, we cannot make a way to achieve God's purpose without His intervention. Therefore, He provided the way for us to enter such a relationship. It is through Jesus alone that we can enter the presence of God. We accept this truth by faith, and through that, can know God personally through Jesus.

When the temple was constructed, God said He would reside in the inner sanctum of the temple called the Holy of Holies. Only the high priest could enter this place and experience the presence of God. When Jesus chose to go to the cross and release His Spirit to death, He said, "It is finished" (John 19:30). He was stating that the work of redemption was complete. Jesus released His Spirit from His earthly body, and that body died. However, His Spirit went into the place of death, called Sheol, and He took the keys of death, Hell, and the grave away from His enemy (and ours), Satan. When He conquered death in this way, Jesus was able to return to life. He rose again, taking up the same body He had left in the tomb. However, at the moment His spirit reentered it, His body took on the form that was victorious over death. Jesus cannot die again. He did it one time because that is all God required. Jesus is the ultimate sacrifice and the only One who fulfilled the requirement of perfection needed for humanity to be ransomed from the chief kidnapper and thief, Satan.

Glory

Jesus crowns us with Himself. It is through Him, and Him alone, that we obtain righteousness, which means we are made right and brought into right relationship with God because of Jesus and His sacrifice. In and of ourselves, we have no righteousness, but through Jesus, we are made righteous. By Him, we can obtain this crown of Life. Because of this righted relationship, we know our prayer and communication with God brings results (James 5:16).

The Lord Crowns us with His Life. It is time for us to understand that when we have entrusted our lives to Him, we are His royal children. He desires we no longer live in fear of any kind but that we live in His power, that we know His love completely, and that we have a sound mind that dwells in His peace.

It is time for you to receive His grace and mercy. It is time for you to recognize His presence in yourself. It is time for you to wear the crown of His Life. It is time for you to set your royal rendezvous with the King of Kings and Lord of Lords, the king of the universe, God, the great I AM. It is time for you to don the royal garments, carry your scepter, let Him place on you the crown of His life, and take your royal place reserved in His kingdom.

Sparkling Joy—The Indelible Mark of Glimmering Life Connection

Not only do we wear the crown of life, but we also become the adornment of the crown of our King. "And the Lord their God will save them on that day as the flock of His people, for they shall be as the [precious] jewels of a crown, lifted high over and shining glitteringly upon His land" (Zech. 9:16 AMP). What a triumphant picture Zechariah paints for us as he portrays God saving His children from their destruction as a loving shepherd protecting his flock. He describes the beauty of knowing that when we deliver ourselves entirely over to God, we become like jewels in His crown. These are not mediocre, run-of-the-mill gemstones, but precious, treasured jewels glistening in the Lord's crown.

Gemstones are classified by several indicators, including physical properties such as hardness, density, color, and luster. These jewels Zechariah described are of the highest quality in every area; strong, solid, bright, clear, and brilliant. Another important gauge for classifying a gemstone is the kind of mark it makes on a streak plate. As gems in the crown of God's Kingdom, we also are identified with the type of mark we leave on the world. Like Zechariah, the prophet Isaiah portrayed God's children as being a crown, "You will also be a crown of beauty [splendor] in the hand of the Lord, and a royal diadem in the hand of your God" (Isa. 62:3 AMP).

The presence of a crown holds unspoken expectation, and a crown in God's hand means we are created to fulfill His purpose. We were not designed to sit back and let life roll by us. We are expected to continue in our pursuit of accomplishing God's purpose. In doing this, we will find we can progress in areas we once thought impossible. We may even be called to resurrect dreams and aspire toward goals we thought were dead to us.

A crown also denotes the perception of nobility, confidence, and strength. As Isaiah continued his message to the people of God, he addressed the reestablished view of their identity, saying, "It will no longer be said to you, 'Forsaken,' Nor to your land will it any longer be said, 'Desolate,' but you will be called, 'My delight is in her,' And your land, 'Married;' For the Lord delights in you, And to Him your land will be married" (Isa. 62:4 AMP). Crowned as children of God, adopted into His family through the sacrifice of Jesus, He gives us a new identity. In it, we are perceived as righteous. We are no longer forsaken, nor desolate and unusable. We are now transformed, beautiful, noble, strong, and made right.

A crown also carries with it the anticipation of a response. Isaiah began his message proclaiming the legacy the people of God would leave on the world, saying, "The nations will see your righteousness, and all kings your glory; And you will be called by a new name Which the mouth of the Lord will designate" (Isa. 62:2 AMP). When we are crowned as God's children, there is the anticipation of blessing and favor of the kingdom of God. We have an opportunity to bring to others the hope of a renewed life that has been given to us.

Because of our transformed mindset and a new identity, others will see the difference in us. They will know that we are changed and filled with joy, grace, and peace. The mark we leave on the world around us will be that of the marvels of God's magnificent presence, and people will want to know how they can attain what we possess. Because of this new name of God's delight, we will be those who are called *lovely* because we deliver the Good News of God's salvation (Isa. 52:7). With this positive connection to life, we will make a significant mark and a positive impact on the world around us. The testimony of our changed life is the witness to others of the good news of God's salvation. That is the legacy we can leave with each encounter.

Making that life connection with The King, we can leave an indelible mark on the world. We will shine the light of the Lord onto the lives of those around us. They will see the sparkle we leave, will take it up themselves, and they will begin to shine with the new life and light of Jesus. Then they will bend that light and sparkle on the world around themselves. Let us pursue our royal rendezvous, make the life connection with The King, and be glistening jewels, sparkling throughout the world for the glory of God.

Notes: Images and Written Works

1. **Webster's American Family Dictionary,** Random House, Inc., New York, NY, 1998.

2. Map of State of Texas obtained at: https://www.tourtexas. com/graphics/maps/texasCities.gif

3. Breyer, Melissa. "The 10 Windiest Cities in the US." 18 May 2016, www.treehugger.com

4. Alice Callahan, Ph.D., The Urban Child Institute, *Domestic Violence: An Unwanted Family Legacy*, October 17, 2014, urbanchildinstitute.org "It turned out that exposure to domestic violence in the first five years of life directly predicted involvement in a violent relationship at age 23, either as a victim or a perpetrator."

5. **Switch on Your Brain: The Key to Peak Happiness, Thinking, and Health.** Dr. Caroline Leaf, Baker Books, 2013 Grand Rapids, MI

6. **Webster's American Family Dictionary,** Random House, Inc., New York, NY, 1998.

7. Assurance of our relationship to God – Rom. 5:8, 8:31-32 & 38-39; Assurance of our identity in Christ – John 1:12; Eph. 1:5; 1 Cor. 6:17; Gal. 3:27-28; Assurance of our place & purpose – Eph. 1:3-14, 2:10; Ps. 139:1-18; Jer. 1:5.

8. Supercharged Affirmations, The Salem New Age Center, Salem, Massachusetts, USA. Accessed August 2007.

9. Affirmations (New Age) – Wikipedia https://en.wikipedia.org/wiki/Affirmations_(New_Age), This page was last edited on 27 December 2018, at 17:36 (UTC).

10. Oxford Dictionary Online, Oxford University Press, en.oxforddictionaries.com/definition/neuroplasticity.

11. Christ is seated at the right hand of the Father – Matt. 22:44; Acts 2:33, 7:55-56; Rom. 8:34; Eph. 1:20; Col. 3:1; Heb. 1:3, 8:1, 10:12, 12:2; Rev. 3:21.

12. Matt. 1:1-17; Lk. 3:23-38

13. Merriam-Webster Online Dictionary © 2015, Merriam Webster Incorporated. "History and Etymology for hypocrite. Middle English *ypocrite*, borrowed from Anglo-French *ipocrite*, borrowed from Late Latin *hypocrita*, borrowed from Greek hypokrites "answerer, actor on a stage, pretender," from hypokri-, variant stem of hypokrinomai, hypokrinesthai, "to reply, make an answer, speak in dialogue, play a part on the stage, feign" -tes, agent suffix"

14. NAZ Exhaustive Concordance of the Bible with Hebrew-Aramaic and Greek Dictionaries © 1981, 1998 The Lockman Foundation.

15. Thayer's Greek Lexicon, electronic database. © 2002, 2003, 2006, 2011, Biblesoft, Inc.

16. Merriam Webster Online Dictionary © 2015, Merriam Webster Incorporated.

About the Author

Leah has been connecting people to redesigned life in Christ for more than thirty-five years. She is an author, speaker, coach, and minister. Along with her husband, Mike, she founded VineSweet Ministries to help overwhelmed people collapse problems of the past and collect the right information about themselves so that they can connect more effectively to life and relationships.

After serving many years as Worship Minister, with the support of Mike—an accomplished musician, Leah currently serves as an Associate Pastor at Amarillo's First Church of the Nazarene.

Throughout her corporate career and in ministry, Leah has observed that many people lead disconnected lives and work without purpose. With a degree in Christian Studies & Biblical Counseling, Leah invests in helping others find the path to genuine life connection. Leah has an exceptional ability to extract relatable teaching points from life experiences to equip and position others to discover their potential, redesign their lives, and fulfill their Kingdom purpose.

Leah is a frequent speaker, inspiring and motivating many to lead a purposeful, well-connected life. She has appeared on television and hosts her radio broadcast *VineSweet Connection*. Leah's weekly vlog *Winning WINS-DAY* is released each Wednesday on social media outlets.

Leah's favorite pastimes are listening to great music—especially worship, modern blues, and smooth jazz—coffee and conversation with friends, and writing beside her mountain stream in Colorado. She loves most of all, spending time with Mike, their children, and grandchildren. The Forts make their home in Amarillo, Texas. They have a daughter, Sydney, who is married to Chase Clark; a son, Lane, who is married to Neeley; and seven grandchildren.

Web: LeahFortConnects.com
Facebook: @VineSweetConnection
Twitter: @LeahFortConnect
LinkedIn: linkedin.com/in/leah-fort

For booking information: bookings@leahfortconnects.com

Connect with
Your Royal Rendezvous
fans and share
your favorite thoughts and quotes from the book
across your social media using
#YourRoyalRendezvous

Celebrate and share your victories using
#ArisefromDefeat

Buried Treasure Workshop

Buried Treasure Workshop guides your group to mine for the gems within enabling you to establish your plan for growth, set your focus to reach your goals, and polish your dreams into reality.

Let Leah help you discover *your* buried treasure and achieve the ultimate, divinely designed vision for your life.

Make the dream of attaining personal and spiritual success reality with the *Buried Treasure Workshop*.

Visit:
LeahFortConnects.com

Your Next Step

It is time for *you* to arise and take your rightful place!

Join Leah each week on *The VineSweet Connection* **broadcast** as you pursue your royal rendezvous. She will lead as you learn practical steps to **Confront** the issues prohibiting you from fulfilling your purpose, **Collapse** and render them powerless, **Collect** right information about yourself in relationship to God in Christ, **Convert** your thinking, and **Connect** to a transformed life in Christ.

What is the cost of staying where you are?

Success awaits your arrival!

The successful life you desire is waiting. You were created to live as a shining jewel in God's crown. Step out of your chains and into your purpose. Start your transformation at LeahFortConnects.com

Bring Leah into Your Organization

Speaker. Author. Minister.

Leah's joyful enthusiasm and authenticity connects her to the heart of your audience. Whether a keynote, conference, or workshop, her message and training will recharge, renew, and refresh your group, while she educates, equips and empowers for a life-changing impact.

Start the Conversation with Leah Today.
https://LeahFortConnects.com
bookings@leahfortconnects.com